Wisdom of the
Buddhist Masters

Robert Sachs has a B.A. in comparative religion and sociology and a Masters in social work. For over 30 years he has studied Eastern spiritual and healing traditions and systems with some of today's greatest living Tibetan and Indian masters. He is a member of the Karma Kagyu school of Tibetan Buddhism and the personal student of H.H. Kunzig Shamar Rinpoche. Robert works to integrate contemporary medical treatment with ancient wisdom in many areas, and is the author of *The Passionate Buddha: Wisdom on Intimacy and Enduring Love* and *The Buddha at War*. He lives in California.

By the same author

Tibetan Ayurveda: Health Secrets From the Roof of the World

The Passionate Buddha: Wisdom on Intimacy and Enduring Love

Perfect Endings: A Conscious Approach to Dying and Death

Rebirth Into Pure Land: A True Story of Birth, Death, and Transformation

The Buddha at War: Peaceful Heart, Courageous Action in Troubled Times

Wisdom of the Buddhist Masters

COMMON AND UNCOMMON SENSE

With a foreword of an excerpt from H.H. Dalai Lama's
Nobel Peace Prize acceptance speech

Edited and with Commentary by
Robert Sachs

WATKINS PUBLISHING
LONDON

Distributed in the United States and Canada by
Sterling Publishing Co., Inc.
387 Park Avenue South, New York, NY 10016-8810

This edition published in the UK 2008 by
Watkins Publishing, Sixth Floor, Castle House,
75–76 Wells Street, London W1T 3QH

1 3 5 7 9 10 8 6 4 2

Designed and typeset by Jerry Goldie

Printed and bound in Great Britain

Library of Congress Cataloging-in-Publication data available

ISBN: 978-1-905857-90-6

For information about custom editions, special sales, premium and
corporate purchases, please contact Sterling Special Sales
Department at 800-805-5489 or specialsales@sterlingpub.com

www.watkinspublishing.co.uk

CONTENTS

Foreword

WORDS FROM H.H. THE FOURTEENTH DALAI LAMA'S
NOBEL PEACE PRIZE SPEECH, 1989

Today we are truly a global family. What happens in one part of the world may affect us all. This, of course, is not only true of the negative things that happen, but is equally valid for the positive developments. We not only know what happens elsewhere, thanks to the extraordinary modern communications technology, we are also directly affected by events that occur far away. We feel a sense of sadness when children are starving in East Africa. Similarly, we feel a sense of joy when a family is reunited after decades of separation by the Berlin Wall. Our crops and livestock are contaminated and our health and livelihood are threatened when a nuclear accident happens miles away in another country. Our own security is enhanced when peace breaks out between warring parties in other continents.

But war or peace; the destruction or the protection of nature; the violation or promotion of human rights and democratic freedoms; poverty or material well-being; the lack of moral and spiritual values or their existence and development; and the breakdown or development of human understanding, are not isolated phenomena that can be analyzed and tackled independently of one another. In fact, they are very much interrelated at all levels and need to be approached with that understanding.

Peace, in the sense of the absence of war, is of little value to someone who is dying of hunger or cold. It will not remove the pain of torture inflicted on a prisoner of conscience. It does not comfort those who have lost their loved ones in floods caused by senseless deforestation in a neighboring country. Peace can only last where human rights are respected, where the people are fed, and where individuals and nations are free. True peace with ourselves and with the world around us can only be achieved through the development of mental peace. The other phenomena mentioned above are similarly interrelated. Thus, for example, we see that a clean environment, wealth or democracy mean little in the face of war, especially nuclear war, and that material development is not sufficient to ensure human happiness.

... Clearly, it is of great importance, therefore, to understand the interrelationship among these and other phenomona, and to approach and attempt to solve problems in a balanced way that takes these different aspects into consideration. Of course it is not easy. But it is of little benefit to try to solve one problem if doing so creates an equally serious new one. So really we have no alternative; we must develop a sense of universal responsibility not only in the geographic sense, but also in respect to the different issues that confront our planet.

Introduction

The presence and relevance of the teachings of the Buddha, both in our search for meaning and facing the stress and strains of modernity, are both obvious and ubiquitous. Its presence can be seen in ordinary pop culture and commercial themes; a hotel chain that can say your visit will be like "nirvana"; a rock group that raps the bodhisattva vows; a restaurant and spa chain of impeccable quality with the seemingly odd name of Buddha Bar. In the West's fascination for personality icons, H.H. the fourteenth Dalai Lama is a spiritual rock star. And there are other contemporary Eastern and Western teachers with large popular followings. Some are even contributors to this book.

For those of more literary tastes, there is the fast-growing body of translated Buddhist texts and teachings of contemporary masters lining the shelves of bookstores, often bestsellers. Issues in the world are briefly discussed in order to launch into the philosophy and practice of Buddhist logic and meditation. Historical or modern examples of the suffering caused by sickness, poverty, and warfare are a backdrop or springboard to embark upon teachings on unconditional, absolute truths and methods offered by Buddhism. For the most part, the emphasis is on the cultivation of the Buddhist practitioner rather on the issues they face per se.

But what if there were a book that put the issues front and center? In everyday terms, what does Buddhism have to say about sickness, poverty, and warfare, beyond the obvious importance of the transformation of the individual? What about social and political action?

What are the opinions of today's teachers on what they see around them? And would Buddhist teachers be willing to "go on record" to give their views and perspectives on the issues? Many Buddhist prayers end with the wish to see an end to sickness, poverty, and warfare. Would teachers be willing to confront these issues in specific terms, and address the rise of fundamentalism, the growing war in the Middle East, global warming, stem cell research, the AIDS epidemic, the world's "addiction" to oil, nuclear proliferation, etc.? Would they be willing to offer practical solutions? And, given the gloom-and-doom perspectives and the thirst for Armageddon that prevails in both the Eastern and Western forms of fundamentalism, do these teachers have a sense as to how the world will look in the next 50 to 100 years?

In my last book, *The Buddha at War*, I was less concerned with specific issues and more focused on a wider perspective; facilitating a kind of daily practice that would help people live a life engaged in the world, politically or socially, at whatever level they felt comfortable. But, in the immediacy of the magnitude of the global problems that bring into question our very survival, the editor-in-chief of Watkins Publishing, Michael Mann, thought that as a sequel to *The Buddha at War*, it would be extremely valuable to solicit the views and guidance of some of the world's most renowned Buddhist teachers and writers.

I felt a sense of urgency to wholeheartedly accept Michael's request and after numerous emails, letters, and phone calls either directly to these teachers or their spokesperson, the answer from most came back saying that they would be happy to "go on record." And that is what this book is all about.

Some readers may want to classify what is said in this volume as Buddhist teaching, although what is shared by these teachers will not be found – for the most part – in the Buddhist canon. I believe that they would prefer us to view their words as Buddhist sensibility; a look at the world and the current issues we face through the lens of minds well practiced in the teaching and methods of the Buddha.

That I seek the views and perspectives of Buddhist masters and scholars on contemporary issues may lead some to assume that this book is about Buddhism, is for Buddhists, or is somehow either not intended for, or of little use to, those who are not within the Buddhist "fold" so to speak. This could not be further from the truth. And such a view in no way understands what Buddhism is.

A dear friend and noted lama, Lama Ole Nydahl, has taught for years that the terms "Buddhism" or "Buddhist" may be relevant to some after discovering and wanting to engage the practices and teachings of the Buddha. Others who are unfamiliar with these teachings and practices may also find the label "Buddhist" to be a useful distinction. But in Tibetan, Lama Ole would say, these terms do not exist. Rather, there are people that live within or follow the teachings, and those that do not. The Buddha's teachings are called the dharma.

Parochially, "dharma" has been translated by Westerners to mean "the truth." But such a translation is poor and inadequate and places the dharma in the same landscape as faith-based or theocentric traditions who lay claim to having "the truth." Such a definition places "Buddhism" on the world stage as one more "ism" that humanity is supposed to embrace or refute depending upon which side of the fence one is standing on. In fact, the defining of dharma as "the truth" and the teachings of the Buddha as being "Buddhism" have not always served the vision and goal of his teachings. In my interview with Christopher Titmuss, and in my concluding chapter, this will be explained more fully. For now, I shall only say that embracing and proclaiming the Buddha's teachings as a world "ism" by those who want to identify themselves as "Buddhists" and others who need to label those practitioners of Buddha's teachings has created bureaucracies and hierarchies that have had their share of scandals and intrigues. No "ism" – in fact no institution, be it social, political, religious, environmental and so on – is ever free of such, and Buddhism is no exception.

Dharma, most appropriately translated, means "the way things are." In the words of Professor Robert Thurman, Siddhartha Gautama was a psychonaut. Having seen in his native India the warfare waged in the name of God, the dissention and bickering over who had the greater connection to or proper understanding of God, he decided to approach his own spiritual awakening from a different angle. If it was true that God was an objective truth, then there should be no disagreement about who He or She was or our respective roles in the order of things. If there *were* disagreements, then these disagreements could have little to do with God, but were more the result of our own biases and desires; our own subjective perspective. Thus, rather than debate or kill for God, wouldn't it be more sensible to examine how we came to this perspective about God and other matters in the first place? Instead of looking outside ourselves, would it not be better to go within and dismantle the mechanisms that lead us to the divergent conclusions that we torment each other with?

So Siddhartha went within, examining the psyche, examining his heart and mind. He used the innate resources of being human to go within and discover the origins of our suffering – individually and collectively – and develop the skillful means and wisdom to free himself and others from that suffering.

In Siddhartha's inner journey, he found that suffering results from the unbridled havoc created by what he termed the Three "Poisons." These "poisons" are *ignorance*, *attachment*, and *aggression*. Simply put, we don't have a full picture of our world or who we really are (ignorance); based on reinforced patterns and reactions, we develop and hold onto erroneous views and perspectives about our world and ourselves (attachment); and we willfully ignore, get defensive, or will even attack those who do not agree with our views and perspectives (aggression).

One can see these poisons at work in our personal lives; health choices, emotional entanglements, and the various soap operas in our lives, even at the spiritual level where sexual guilt imposed by puritanical dogmas literally sucks the life blood out of our relationships or gives us a delusional peace of mind and a promise of having 100 virgins at our beck and call in heaven if we strap bombs on our bodies and detonate ourselves in a marketplace. At the spiritual level especially, the poisons become most toxic; we can expand out into our social and political spheres and look at the heinous results of such doctrines as manifest destiny and jihad. Spiritual hubris can be the basis upon which we ignore the warning signs and deny our part in global warming. A belief in predestination or an infantile understanding of karma can cause some to ignore preventative measures; to avoid seeking treatment for AIDS or take seriously the necessity to clean up the River Ganges.

The Buddha's inner journey led him to create methods to dismantle and transform these three poisons. The goal is to develop the skill, wisdom, and resourcefulness of being to live a peaceful, happy life, extended to the world, based on an understanding of the connectedness of all life, mutual respect, and an encouragement for each and every being to discover their own innate potentials to "be all that they can be." The dharma, therefore, is an understanding of the problems inherent in being alive, mapping out these problems so that they are demystified and seen for what they are. It provides practical psychophysical practices and recommendations for ethical action to address these problems. Until we are aware of the subtleties and depth of our con- nectedness to all that is seen and unseen, we may need to take certain premises on faith, and thus – when disaster seems most likely – choose our actions based on external, moralistic guidelines. But, in the end, if we are to grow, moralistic action and faith must give way to a certainty based on experience from within rather than force from without. If our actions continue to be based on rigidly enforced codes and externally reinforced edicts, our behaviour will be stiff and twisted and our minds will seek to revolt by means of a variety of perversions that can be harmful to us and to others. Thus, those who practice and live dharma should exhibit signs of being spontaneous, joyful, resourceful, connected. Love and compassion are the bases of their action; having a passion and affection for life and participating in making the world a viable, sustainable place for ourselves and future generations.

Described in this way, "Buddhism" has *no dogma* other than the assertion that each of us possess buddha-nature. It is our honest, sincere, and determined endeavor to understand ourselves, reach our full potential, and act with an altruistic intention in the world, that will bring our humanity to its greatest fruition, i.e. awakening or enlightenment. That said, it should be clear that any other path that brings about the same results is as much Buddhist as that which is merely labeled as such. In that way, I am reminded of how H.H. Dalai Lama saw in the Trappist father, Thomas Merton, a man who showed the determination and qualities that are the goal of Buddhist practice. And, when years later I had the opportunity to visit Father Merton's monastery in Trappist, Kentucky, I had fascinating discussions with Catholic brothers who practiced yoga and Buddhist meditation in their cells. As far as they were concerned, these were great methods to help them get closer to God.

Many in the modern Western world assume that because the teachings of the Buddha have such a strong emphasis on peace and peacefulness, that "Buddhism" is synonymous with pacifism. Some go so far as to believe Buddhism has more of a "hands-off," do nothing, or "whatever-will-be-will-be" approach to life and its problem. Even from within, those who claim to be Buddhist will sometimes hold to this notion. To my mind, such an understanding of so-called Buddhists comes out of an immature understanding of karma and/or being white, middle-class spiritual shoppers who have the leisure to philosophize and do not have the stomach or will to get their hands dirty.

Pacifism may be embraced as a Buddhist approach if it is the sane, logical, and prudent approach to take in a given situation. Throughout Asia, Buddhist counsel and sensibility have historically been sought to de-escalate and make sense of social and political realities and conflicts. In the history of the world – whilst there have been and still continue to be vestiges of egoic conflicts amongst Buddhist sects – there has never been a war waged or an imperialistic campaign embarked on in the name of the Buddha or Buddhism. Even today in America, we find, for example, someone like Professor Robert Thurman being listed as one of the 25 most influential thinkers in America, bringing a sane, peaceful, and inspiring vision to what America can become.

At the same time, this does not exhaust or deny other methods – even a path that includes conflict. For peace is not necessarily about the ending of war or hostility. This is a by-product. Rather peace, real peace, is *the transformation of the human heart* – a turning from what is habitual and instinctual from the standpoint of less fortunate realms or dimensions of existence to a true and natural realization of the loving nature inherent in being human. Thus it is that my interview with H.H. Kunzig Shamar Rinpoche goes boldly beyond our normal sensibilities to speak of the necessity to sometimes wage what he describes as "white" wars. And remember, after the completion of these interviews we have witnessed the civil protests led by Buddhist monks in Myanmar as an example of Buddhist activism.

As shown earlier, the Three Poisons are not just at play in matters of war and conflict within or between societies. Thus the Buddhist masters and thinkers interviewed for this book have taken their understanding and sensibility of dharma and aimed it squarely at some of the thorniest issues we face in these times. What you shall find in these interviews will – I am certain – be interesting, awakening, and thought-provoking. But as wisdom and compassion have many sides and have little to do with conservative sensibility, liberal fluffiness, or political correctness, you may find yourself sometimes shocked by their candor.

So be it. I make no apologies for the words of enlightened masters and deep thinkers. If we are to see a different world, a transformed world, we have to roll up our sleeves and get dirty. These teachers have committed themselves. And, at this point, if we are truly desirous of seeing things differently, we have no choice but to become committed as well. I wish to thank each of the teachers who participated: H.H. Kunzig Shamar Rinpoche, Ven. Tarthang Tulku Rinpoche, Geshe Tenzin

Wangyal Rinpoche, Geshe Michael Roach and his consort, Christie McNally, Ven. Ajahn Amaro, Roshi Joan Halifax, Ven. Thubten Chodron, Tenzin Robert Thurman, and Christopher Titmuss. There were also many other teachers I approached who, for any number of reasons, said they could not participate in this project. To all of them, I also want to express my gratitude for being willing to receive and respond to my emails and letters.

Thanks also to Michael Mann of Watkins for encouraging me to embark on this journey. This is the first time I have been approached to write something as a commission, and it was a challenge. Yet the idea was so exhilarating, I couldn't help but want to jump in and make it happen.

Of course and always, my heart of gratitude goes to my beloved, Melanie. Together for 33 years, the ride gets only more beautiful and amazing.

Although my wish is that this book be read in all parts of the world, more than likely it will circulate in countries where there is a higher degree of affluence and a social and political climate where there is more peace than constant strife. If this fits your situation, consider yourself lucky – or karmically blessed. If you believe in reincarnation, consider that you got there because of previous good deeds. If you don't believe in karma or reincarnation, it doesn't matter. You are still better off than most of the people in the world.

With that in mind, if you hold to the notion that "what you sow, so you shall reap," you are being called upon. If you have any love for another or for future generations, there is no choice but to get involved. For your bliss to be real, for your bliss to go beyond just the temporary here and now, you need to think of others. There is nothing else to do, but that.

Your first step is to get informed – so read on…

Going Up the Mountain

Although I have been close to all of the teachers who were interviewed for this book, either as a student or from other meetings, this does not mean to say that it was easy to arrange the interviews that follow. Spiritual teachers of note in this world are like other public figures. They have a close circle of associates – usually disciples – who take care of their administration, sometimes even their more personal needs. Their schedules are tight and their presence is in demand. At the same time, they need to do those things that give them their spiritual understanding; they need to have time to themselves, to meditate, pray, and gather the necessary energy and strength to keep up with the pace of their lives, to pursue the tasks for – in the words of Buddhist dedication prayers, "the benefit of all sentient beings." As such, each of these teachers has their own domain – and they have what I describe as "guard dogs" who rightly guard and monitor access.

If access is granted, when approaching such teachers, it is usually wise to come prepared. Thus, like the stories of going up the mountain to ask the wise man at the summit about the meaning of life or what one should do with the rest of one's life, I wanted to be certain and clear about what I was going to ask them. I did not want to waste, or feel that I was wasting their precious time, for rarely does one get a second chance.

The questions generally asked of these teachers in both private and public settings range from the profoundly mystical ("What is the meaning of life?") to the most mundane ("Should I quit my job?"). For the most part, it appears to me that they speak of what is ultimately useful: how to develop wisdom and compassion in one's daily life. Few take much time to dwell or comment upon current events or geopolitics, apart from some of the younger Western teachers. The Tibetan reincarnates, on the other hand, up until a century ago, were from a culture where people lived, moved around, and died within five miles of where they were born. This has been the dominant paradigm of the human species for thousands of years. If natural or man-made events precipitated the collapse of a local ecosystem, people would abandon their homes to seek new resources. If nomadic – as is the case of many of the families of Tibetan teachers – the seasons would roll around and they would come back to their spring, summer, fall, and winter residences over the course of the years.

But in these days, our human family has outgrown these as suitable options. With the population over 6 billion on the planet, the nomadic life of tribes has all but vanished with the needs of a global population spiraling out of control. Those who once lived provincial, close-to-home lives are being taunted by and tempted with images brought to them over the airwaves via radio and television and a burgeoning information superhighway of internets and cellular technology. And a growing number take to the roads, the seas, the skies with forms of transportation that make it possible to have breakfast in New York, lunch in Paris, and supper in Istanbul. The solution most often adopted for meeting the material and survival needs of this bustling, expanding population has been industrialization, spanning nations and continents, resulting in the blurring of nation-states, and the emergence of over-regulated governments usually closely aligned to corporate structures deemed most suitable for managing resources. And, because we have not yet tamed the human tendencies of greed and self-interest, political intrigue and wars are sprouting in every corner of the planet.

In the face of this, our modernity, and the problems, challenges, and dangers that have arisen, global and geopolitical questions have become more relevant to our daily sense of place and well-being on the planet. The existential approach or absolutisms of spiritual advice – whilst still, if not more, useful than ever – need to be augmented with answers to tough questions if we are to avert what some view as a path leading to Armageddon, or the end of days brought on by man-made or natural disasters. When survival becomes an imperative, unless one subscribes to a fatalistic, predetermined, or nihilistic philosophy, spiritual advice needs to be real and immediate. In this I am reminded of Mahatma Gandhi when he said, "For a starving man, God comes in the form of bread."

And so, I wanted to come to these Buddhist masters and teachers with questions normally not presented or discussed over the course of weekend dharma classes and seminars. What I decided to do was approach each teacher not from the standpoint of a Buddhist practitioner per se, but rather as a consumer of popular media who may have read about Buddhism. I wanted to ask questions on things that I had read in *USA Today*, heard from liberal and conservative talk-show pundits, or seen on network evening news. My idea was to ask about the big topics and stories spun this way and that: terrorism, fundamentalism, jihad, global warming, SARS, AIDS, Darfur, etc.

The following is the questionnaire I came up with.

QUESTIONNAIRE

Wisdom from the Masters for the 21st Century

A DARK AGE

Some years ago, many Buddhist teachers spoke about the historical Buddha's prediction of this being the time of a dark age. From your understanding and perspective:

1 what is a dark age?
2 what signs or conditions exist that would indicate that we are in a dark age?
3 what attitude should we as humans take on this situation? And, how can we best cultivate the attitude that will best serve us and help in the transformation of these dark times?

SICKNESS, POVERTY, AND WARFARE

Please focus on the two questions in this section as a main essay that you will contribute to the book.

Sickness, poverty, and warfare have seemingly been present on this planet since early times. There have been times where these were less or greater in some places more than others, and in some times more than others.

1 From your perspective, which one of these three stands out as the most significant at this time or possibly for all time? How does it impact or contribute to the other two?

2 The causes and conditions that come together to create sickness, poverty, and warfare are both individual and collective.

   a What do those who are faced with the experience of grave sickness or poverty, or who are in the midst of warfare need to address within themselves to cope with and transform their suffering?

   b What actions can individuals take to lessen the suffering of those around them who may be suffering from similar conditions?

   c At the social and political levels, what do you see as the responsibilities of governments in addressing these conditions?

Being more specific – please feel free to choose whichever questions in this section you would most like to address. Doing several would be great as we then get the perspectives of many teachers, so be generous with your answers if you can.

Much media attention is given to various specific issues that relate to sickness, poverty, and warfare. Would you be so kind as to add some perspective and understanding on these various matters that seem so dominant in these days? Would you also be willing to comment on what you see as being needed from within (i.e. personally) and without (i.e. collectively from the standpoint of a social, economic, and political perspective) to bring positive changes for the future of the 21st century?

SICKNESS

1 **Drug addiction and drug abuse:** Many governments are worried about the spreading of this problem in all ages and sectors of the population. What factors do you think contribute to this problem? How can we build societies where the need for such drug use is made less?

2 **AIDS and other pandemics such as SARS, avian flu:** Plagues are nothing new on this planet. Some have said that the reasons for them arising are because of religious transgressions. Others have looked at social, economic, and hygiene factors. What do you see as the most sensible way of looking at and working towards eliminating these pandemics?

3 **Malnutrition:** Millions of people are currently starving across the planet. From what you have seen, what are the most significant outer or global factors contributing to this problem? What are the steps that need to be taken to address this problem? How can the average individual contribute to supporting the necessary changes?

The future of medicine

4 The issues of cloning and stem cell research have become controversial. The controversy seems to be in the sphere of religious ethics and beliefs about how life can be created and destroyed and/or used for helping others. What is the Buddhist view on this matter?

   a As classical texts speak of life being conceived via a womb or from an egg, how are those beings created in a test tube, and then implanted into a uterus, perceived? Are they sentient in the same way as other forms of birth?

   b stem cell research and its applications?

POVERTY

The disparity between those who have and those who do not have grows daily. In general, a very small number of people in the world control the world's economies. For the most part, the greatest wealth on this planet is produced from energy sources (mostly oil), the arms trade, drugs (which includes illicit or illegal drugs, pharmaceuticals, alcohol, and coffee), and human trafficking (i.e. the sex trade and pornography).

5 What do you see as the factors that contribute most to poverty?

6 There are various forms of government that exist around the planet. Is one any better than another in helping to bring about the elimination of poverty in today's global economy?

7 What steps could such a government take in bringing about a change in the disparity between the rich and the poor?

8 How can we best utilize and preserve our natural resources? The most important ones at this time seem to be oil and water.

WARFARE

Fundamentalism is on the rise, both in the East and in the West. Some believe that the conflicts in the Middle East and elsewhere have both an economic and religious component. The economic component revolves around oil and other strategic resources. The religious has to do with the conflict between Islam and Christianity that started during the time of the Crusades. That being said…

9 what do you think is the cause for the growth of fundamentalist faiths at this time?

10 what significance does it play in the current conflicts? Do you perceive it as a primary cause or merely a justification for political and economic exploitation?

11 what is the best way to approach or cope with the rising prevalence of this type of faith in communities, and its influence on society?

12 how can conscious parents protect their children from
    proselytizing and the growing popular belief, especially in the
    US, in Armageddon and the end of days?

Terrorism is a term that is hard to define, but used quite liberally by
current Western governments. For the most part, the mention of it
breeds fear.

13 How would you define terrorism?
14 What is a terrorist act?
15 In our current world situation, how would you identify who a
    terrorist is?
16 Can you give examples of persons, organizations, or nations
    who you would define as carrying out terrorist actions,
    without being specific in name?
17 What is the best approach that people of influence or power
    can make to curb or put an end to terrorism?
18 What is the view that will best help ordinary citizens cope with
    the presence of terrorism in their midst?

During World War II and in other wars, good people have often
found themselves living in countries in which they oppose their
government's actions. Many in the US feel that they are witnessing the
rise of a more fascist style of government that bears little resemblance
to the ideals of democracy to which this country was intended to
aspire.

19 What is the attitude and courses of action that would be most
    in keeping with Buddhist ethics?

ENVIRONMENTAL FACTORS

Many scientific studies point to the diminishing of our planet's ozone, global warming, and the rise of air and water pollution. A conference sponsored by former President Bill Clinton on "Global Warming and National Security" warned that without seriously addressing global warming – in particular – over the next few years by limiting and reducing the formation of greenhouse gases, within 70 years the world's oceans could rise by three to seven feet. This would displace millions of people around the globe who live close to shorelines.

1 What do you see as the role of individual responsibility in addressing environmental and ecological concerns?

2 In what ways can individuals contribute to helping change the direction of powerful individuals, governments, and corporations who contribute to this problem?

Finally, please comment on these last five questions.

3 Over the next 100 years, how do you see the people of Earth dealing with these issues? Do you foresee some being resolved more easily than others? Which ones do you see being resolved? Which ones do you think will persist?

4 If you were to gaze into the future to the year 2106, what do you see human society and our planet looking like?

5 If your view is positive, what do you think will contribute to those positive changes over the next 100 years?

6 If you see that we are still in for dark times, what do you think will contribute to that?

7 What would be your final words of encouragement for us as human forms of sentient life in these uncertain times?

The interviews conducted happened in a variety of ways between the spring of 2006 through February 2007. I interviewed H.H. Kunzig Shamar Rinpoche at his dharma center in Menlo Park, California. Geshe Tenzin Wangyal Rinpoche was on tour in Berkeley, where I caught up with him at a student's home. Ven. Tarthang Tulku Rinpoche, who had not granted an interview for over 30 years, was willing to look at the questionnaire and send me answers to the questions he felt most pressing. The rest of the teachers, Geshe Michael Roach and his consort-wife Christie McNally, Ven. Ajahn Amaro, Ven. Thubten Chodron, Tenzin Robert Thurman, and Christopher Titmuss, I managed to catch by phone or Skype in their residences or whilst on the road. With the exception of Ven.Tarthang Tulku Rinpoche, I recorded the interviews, transcribed them, sent them back for revisions or clarifications, and then printed them.

Sometimes there seemed to be ample time, sometimes it was restricted for any number of reasons. Whilst theoretically it may have been neater if each teacher answered every question, I found each had their own interest or expertise, and hence addressed some questions more than others. It also became clear that the answer to one question sometimes negated the reason for asking another. I am not a seasoned investigative reporter, and, whilst I could have been more insistent or disciplined in getting answers to each and every question, this would have been rather contrived.

In the end, I just followed their lead. All had seen the questionnaire at least one to two weeks before. Each of them knew what I wanted. And to my mind, they offered such amazing gems of insights, that there is no way I can look at any of the interviews and think they could have been better than they are.

The interviews, as you will read them, are minimally edited and are rather conversational. I think this makes them real. At one point, I thought that I would ask one question and create a "round table" of answers. This became impossible for a number of reasons. For one thing, each teacher made comments that literally begged follow-up.

Thus, there would have been endless cuts and digression and the full impact of what they were saying could have been lost. Some of the responses challenge conventional reality, sometimes morality and political correctness. Thus, by keeping the interviews separate, you will know who to applaud or get upset with.

Because of the nature of the questions, current events in "real time" are ever present. I do not think this dates the book, but rather puts it into context. I feel confident that readers of this book in 30 to 40 years' time will actually have a more profound appreciation for what these teachers say, as they will know some of the roots of what they are facing in their own time.

Following the interviews, we shall go "down the mountain" where I will attempt to bring the nuggets, or most salient points of what they have shared, together in a vision of what we shall have to face and what actions we must embrace to survive and grow, both individually and collectively, in this coming century. Based on the insights gleaned from this precious experience, I would like to share my own observations, and hopefully contribute to a dialogue that I hope continues in homes, dharma centers, cafes, government offices, and places of learning everywhere.

The Interviews

H.H. Kunzig
Shamar Rinpoche

ABOUT H.H. KUNZIG SHAMAR RINPOCHE

Mipham Chokyi Lodro was born in Derge, Tibet. At the age of four he was recognized by the 16th Karmapa, Rangjung Rigpe Dorje, as the 14th Shamarpa reincarnation. Upon the Karmapa's request the Tibetan government withdrew its 159-year-old ban of the Shamarpas.

Kunzig Shamar Rinpoche remained with the 16th Karmapa until his death in 1981. He received the entire cycle of Kagyu teachings from the 16th Karmapa. Since the 16th Karmapa's death, Kunzig Shamar Rinpoche has devoted his efforts to the many projects initiated by the late 16th Karmapa. He has completed the reprinting of the "Tengyur," a body of 214 volumes in which prominent Indian and Tibetan masters elucidate the teachings given by the historical Buddha Sakyamuni. Shamar Rinpoche also supports and offers guidance to Rumtek Monastery, the seat of the 16th Karmapa. He co-founded and brought into being the Karmapa International Buddhist Institute, New Delhi,

India. The Institute currently offers courses in Buddhist studies for both monastic and lay students.

Shamar Rinpoche frequently travels abroad where he teaches at the many Kagyu centers worldwide. He also plans to establish an institute for higher Buddhist studies and a retreat center in Nepal.

I first met H.H. Kunzig Shamar Rinpoche in the spring of 1981 in his first visit to the United States. My wife and I both developed a close spiritual and personal relationship with Rinpoche over time. In fact, he gave one of our daughters, Shamara, her Buddhist name. To this day, he remains my main spiritual mentor. My interview with Rinpoche took place in the spring of 2006 at his main center on the United States West Coast in Menlo Park, California.

THE INTERVIEW

Robert: What is a dark age?

Rinpoche: Dark age is when a majority of the people don't have wisdom; they are shallow, have much superstition and follow bad views. One has no intuition how to improve mankind's compassion or to create a peaceful way, and people are always fighting for their own gain.

But this is not really a dark age.

American people who are as old as senior George Bush, his generation, they still had the influence from previous wise generations, professors and politicians from this country as well as Europe, very thoughtful with clear judgment with sharp common sense – so when it came to the Second World War, they didn't make many mistakes. Junior George Bush's generation however, have grown up very comfortably. American kids are very comfortable. Many of his generation became irresponsible and thus choose a life different from normal society. This has made them quite naive. Then the schools became naive as did the teachers. Nowadays, people in the US do not have spontaneous clear judgment. They are more machine-minded. Although I do not speak English as a native English speaker, I have created this phrase, which I think is really true. They are very shallow in their judgment and are making a lot of mistakes. For example, people in this country criticize this current president; that he unnecessarily made this war [referring to Iraq]. No doubt he has made mistakes, but he is also served and informed from other people in the government who are also machine-minded.

A court must be like a machine, otherwise a court cannot exercise the law equally. But, outside of the courts, people should have common sense. They should not act in such a legalistic way. When students go to the universities in the US, what they study seems to make them lead lives that are not quite balanced. At least 30 percent of what they learned should be designed for them to develop spontaneous wisdom. This is what they need. But, they don't get this kind of education so they become machine-like, with little common sense. I think a majority of the people in the US have poor judgment.

Robert: So Rinpoche, if we have not yet entered into a dark age …

Rinpoche: If such machine-minded ways continue and people become more naive, this situation that I am describing can, in two to three generations, invite a dark age.

Robert: In this naivety and lack of judgment that you see, in terms of warfare, there is a rise of fundamentalism. Some look at the problems we are facing in terms of economics and politics. Others see a religious component, particularly between Christianity and Islam, that began as far back as the Crusades. What do you think causes this fundamentalism?

Rinpoche: This is a dangerous situation. My observation is that naivety is growing both in the East and the West. More and more people are becoming more technically minded. As more become technically minded, like a computer, if you give a strong order, people will follow – like machines.

Some time ago, there were rigid Islamic leaders who were fearful of modern ways. They thought that the modern world and its ways would threaten their religious authority. And so they became more insistent that people follow what they were teaching them very strictly. They were successful, but what they learned was that some of the influences of the modern ways were actually helping them. They learned that when young people are more technically minded, they are less intelligent, more superstitious, more unquestioning, and easier to influence. They don't ask why.

The same is true here in America. Students here cannot trace back anything. They do not reflect or analyze how things have evolved to where they are. They cannot trace back anything. Something happening now, they cannot trace back to the cause. They just follow, like water winding which does not go back. Their minds are like water, water going over a slope, never going back, just rushing forward over the slope, never going back.

So, the same is happening in the Middle East with the young people. They are very technically minded. It is very easy to convince them, like how Bin Laden convinced them to fly planes into the Twin Towers in New York, saying things like "very good, very good that you serve the wishes of God." He emphasized this way of thinking to help fixate their minds on doing this deed. Doing things like this, achieving the same result is accomplished by the preachers in the Middle East, taking advantage of this way of thinking and superstition. So these two things, this technical mind plus superstition come easily together to create religious fanatics.

Robert: So, Rinpoche, you are saying that the growth of these fanatics comes from some people having very little education

being fed, by preachers and other influential people, ideas
about the past and tradition, instilling fear and giving them
bad ideas, but that there are also others who, having been given
mostly a technological education, are machine-minded – as
you call it – so are easily trained.

Rinpoche: Modern education system does not improve skill of
judgment of students. Modern education in USA is making students
like machines, so there is no advice on how to be thoughtful, like
Thomas Jefferson, who emphasized that people develop common
sense.

Robert: And education?

Rinpoche: Yes. Gradually, this kind of education has been lost to more
and more technical education in colleges and universities. This makes
the majority of students like machines and their common sense and
judgment decreases. Without clear judgment these youth can be misled
by superstition and the manipulations of politicians.

Like several years back, there was the former military president of
Pakistan [General Zia ul-Haq] who, while he was ruling and before he
was killed in a plane crash, made an Islamic system of government that
used religion as a way of manipulating people to do exactly what he
wanted of them.

Robert: Do you think this fundamentalism is being used to
manipulate political and economic situations?

Rinpoche: Oh, sure. It reminds me of a recent story of a famous
Buddhist teacher in China [the head of Falun Gong] who told people
that he was creating a chakra in their stomach to destroy all their bad
karmas. He would also place an aura behind a person's head which
would protect them from samsara [i.e. conditioned existence]. After he

did these things, he told people that if they did not follow him, he would take these two energies back and they would become helpless. So people immediately believed that they got this protection from him and to not lose it, they would do anything he says. In a few years he had over 250 million disciples in China, about a third of the population of China. He could have easily taken over all of China because of his preaching, and become a very serious religious dictator.

Looking at today's younger US politicians with their machine-minded understanding, some are fixated on this notion of religious freedom. Rather than judging what kind of religion, what a teacher is teaching, there is a blind obedience to the idea of religious freedom. There is no judgment here, just a fixed-mind perspective. In the case of Falun Gong, the Chinese government banned Falun Gong, and these naive American politicians protested and supported the leader of Falun Gong on the base of the fixed idea of religious freedom. The politicians that judged against China this way do not have clear judgment.

I compare this to senior George Bush. He had very clear judgment when he attacked Iraq and subdued Saddam Hussein's ambitions to extend his power. He let Hussein be there as a leader in order to do many good things, although he was not a good person. There were some good results from him just being left where he was. This thoughtful and creative judgment on the part of George Bush senior came from his own mind, not from some book he studied at university.

But the current George Bush is using what he either learned from books he studied at university or Christian books, God's books. That's all.

Robert: So the wisdom is not there in George W Bush's situation.

Rinpoche: No, there is no spontaneous judgment, I don't see it. Really, I am not that interested in politics. But, I am interested in American people's mind power. At this time, Americans and how they are being led is very naive.

Robert: Rinpoche, one of the things I observe locally is that more and more people are fundamentalist and there is a growing influence of fundamentalism in the community. What is the best way to approach people like that?

Rinpoche: Professors and teachers need to teach people to have common sense. That is what is needed. I am not saying that everyone is naive, but this way is growing and if it continues as it is right now, there will be some very grave mistakes made in the future. It will create disasters in this country. Right now, the US government is leading by virtue of the good system that was created for them earlier by very wise leaders. So right now, it is not the people in government who are leading, but rather the system that is leading. The system survives, but without wise people to lead the system, there can be big mistakes.

Robert: The system that was created was very good, but the people that are running it do not know how to use it properly?

Rinpoche: Not quite. More that the system is leading [has a life of its own] and is working fairly well, but if people remain naive with machine minds, there will be big problems in the future. That can happen here. I am very worried that in the future someone here in this country will explore the development of even more serious weapons, because they think that is what they are supposed to do because they are thinking like robots.

Robert: There are people, Rinpoche, who do run things, who think as you describe and have a view that is based on their fundamentalist faith. They believe in Armageddon and that if they don't get what they want, then God can have it back anyway.

Rinpoche: In general, bad things are created by evil-minded people. In the past, like during the time of the world wars, there were people like Hitler and Stalin who intentionally created problems. But that way, where evil-minded people can do such things, is pretty much subdued in this world now. Like the US, and US government is pretty positive. None of the people [like Hitler or Stalin] are around in powerful positions with those kind of intentions. I mean, people can have those kind of intentions, but we are not really in any danger of them taking over. But now, because of naivety and poor judgment, serious mistakes with grave consequences can take place.

Robert: So you don't see what is happening being deliberate or coming about because of evil intention, but more out of a naivety.

Rinpoche: Yes, yes.

Robert: Like walking into a situation without seeing it properly.

Rinpoche: Yes, without seeing properly and acting like a robot. In this way, serious mistakes can be made, especially by the US because it has so much power.

Robert: If this robot or machine mind is the result of and caught up in technology, if you were to look at the education systems in America, what would you encourage to balance this tendency?

Rinpoche: Teachers and professors should teach their students to become thoughtful, to employ more common sense. A court-like mind only judges things based on material facts. But, in normal life, you have to make judgments based on common sense, even if there is not materialistic proof. You cannot understand human nature just by using materialistic proof. You have to rely on more "invisible" sciences to know and understand human nature. Human nature cannot be examined like how you examine metal objects. As humans, we can create and do many things without first relying on materialist proofs. You need to develop judgment.

A crafty human can hide a lot of what they are doing until they finally do what they have set out to do. Then it is too late. That is why Bin Laden could hit the Twin Towers.

Robert: Because so much can be hidden.

Rinpoche: So, if you can only believe things if there are materialist, tangible proofs, then you cannot believe in what is hidden. You only believe it when it happens. In this case, you only believe once the Towers are hit. Then it is too late.

Robert: Do you think 9/11 was the robot or machine mind that was looking for evidence rather than trusting intuition?

Rinpoche: Yes.

Robert: And therefore, if I do not see it, I cannot believe that it is possible.

Rinpoche: In the East, when Asian professors examine a letter, they look at the surface meaning and the underlying meaning. We are educated, by reading one time, to look at what is written and understand what is the hidden meaning that often gets used later as the justification. Many of my American and European friends have no way to understand that hidden meaning. I explain and I point it out to them:

"Look, it is right here. Here is the surface meaning and underneath there is another one." But they do not see it. So I have experience of seeing how mind is trained like a machine.

Robert: Regarding terriorism. [See written questions.] How would you define terrorism?

Rinpoche: When people become naive, religious preachers can use that naivety to convince these people to commit suicide for killing others, with the promise that as a result they will go to heaven. These people have no judgment, so they believe what these preachers say. If you do not have those kind of believers, how can there be terrorism? How could you create those kind of terrorists? Who is willing to waste one's own life just to fight under some politician's order? Who would sacrifice their own life based on someone else's interest?

Robert: So it all comes back to that naivety.

Rinpoche: One hundred percent *yes*.

Robert: Sometimes people will say that that person is a terrorist for what they are doing but they don't necessarily understand that others could see it another way. For example – in the case of the American involvement in the Middle East – from the standpoint of some people in Islamic countries, some view what America is doing as terrorism.

Rinpoche: Sometimes philosophers teach very naively. Sometimes the logic that they use is rubbish logic. What makes what America is doing terrorism?

Robert: Why are people saying that?

Rinpoche: Yes.

Robert: There have been examples in American history where
the US government has used covert soldiers to create chaos.
For example, during the time of the Kennedy administration,
there was a covert operation to undermine the government of
Fidel Castro. They sent soldiers in, unknown to the Cubans,
and they blew up hospitals and other buildings and caused lots
of problems. In response, the Cubans contacted the Russians
which precipitated the Cuban Missile Crisis. So the Cubans
saw the Americans as terrorists. Would the Cubans be justified
in this view? Or what if an Iraqi family – in today's situation –
has American soldiers come into their house thinking that
there is al-Qaeda, and take away members of the family or
possibly even kill them, would the Iraqi family be justified in
calling Americans terrorists?

Rinpoche: If the American soldiers did that intentionally, then yes, you
could call it terrorism.

Robert: OK, then if it is an intentional act, it is one thing, but if
it is just in the course of war and it is not intended, then it is
not terrorism.

Rinpoche: In all times, military people have to follow orders. They
cannot think a lot. Military should be more or less like that. Otherwise,
you cannot fight well. If you have a bunch of philosophers in the
field, you cannot fight well. Soldiers are suppose to be machine-mind-
like. At the same time, the leaders must be thoughtful to prevent
something bad from happening. They must exercise judgment and be
able to anticipate situations before they occur. Nowadays, however, the
leaders are not like that and this is a big mistake.

Robert: So again it comes back to intention. If the intention of whoever is leading the army is to catch something before something bad happens, the intention is good, although the action can be a problem. But this is not terrorism. Terrorism is deliberately creating a problem.

Rinpoche: Terrorism is not really well focused even on creating a desired result. I think of these suicide bombers, and what they believe is like how the early Christian Church tortured people because they did not follow God. That kind of thinking is terrorism.

Robert: Americans watch on TV, videotapes of groups in Iraq holding hostages, threatening to behead them if their demands are not met. They believe that this action will undermine the Americans or shake their confidence. So their intention is that if they do this they further the cause of getting the Americans to leave.

Rinpoche: Let me give you an example: the disease smallpox. Smallpox kills people. In order to cure people, one approach is to bring up the smallpox in what we Tibetans call a "white" way. We call it "white" smallpox. If you give white smallpox to the people, then the black changes to the white. Initially, it makes you sick, but it is not fatal. It stops you from dying. If you did not do this, the "black" kind would come by itself and people would die. So you are forcing them to the surface. In order to prevent big danger from happening, sometimes you have to instigate something, then everything will come out and can be dealt with.

So, using your example of when Americans sent soldiers into Cuba, the master plan may have been to make the Cubans prematurely get the Russians into the situation, so they could be confronted and easily stopped. Otherwise, perhaps slowly and smartly, the Cubans would have gotten the Russians to put missiles in; the situation would have been much worse. So this is not terrorism. This is a skillful method.

Robert: During World War II and other times, sometimes people find themselves living in countries where they do not agree with what the government is doing. There were good people in Germany that did not like what Hitler was doing. There were good people in Russia that did not like what Stalin was doing. Right now, there are many Americans who do not like what the American government is doing, especially in Iraq. What attitude and course of action should such people take, that would be in keeping with Buddhist principles? If you disagree with what your government is doing, how should you try to influence the situation?

Rinpoche: I don't know enough to say whether George Bush's attacking Iraq was a mistake or not. But, in the beginning, he did say that there were weapons of mass destruction there. After that, it was found that they were not there. Then, he said he was going to restore democracy in Iraq and that was the reason why he attacked. That is not a good reason. But, nowadays, the American people are – I am sorry to say – not very thoughtful. They did not know how to respond to what he said as his reasons. Actually, in that case, if America wants to support democracy in Iraq, they cannot support the current leader of Pakistan, Musharraf, because he, too, is a dictator. So America will have to go to war with every country in the world where there is marshal law. But George Bush prevailed because no one, or the majority of the people, did not know how to respond to his reasoning.

George Bush's claim that he attacked Iraq to restore democracy there is not a good reason. If there had been weapons of mass destruction, then fine. Or, if the strategy is to liberate and democratize the entire Middle East and Saddam Hussein is considered the biggest blockage, and then the US democratizes Iraq as a first step and then liberates all the people in the Middle East region who are suffering under dictatorships, OK, then fine, maybe that's alright. But if that is the case, why wouldn't you start with Iran first instead of Iraq?

I think that this war is just an interest to a very few people who are interested in the money they can get from oil. Because why?

I have come across, and sometimes confronted, many journalists and book-writers on how they lie. Many of them do lie. [An example that we can all relate to.] When we were children, when we did not want to study, we said we were sick. Later on we do become sick. So, even though we were not sick at the time we said we were, now that we are, can anyone argue with us? Supposedly book-writers (unless you write fiction) and journalists are not supposed to tell lies. But sometimes they lie intentionally and sometimes unintentionally. You take on the opinion or the information of another person and maybe it's not true, or you misunderstood but you did not intentionally lie. Maybe you really thought that way and you were convinced. But people really don't know one way or the other. Maybe they know that what you are writing is a lie, but believe in you to think that you actually believe that you are not lying.

So you want to attack Iraq for petrol, instead you use the media and journalists to spread the message that you are attacking because of weapons of mass destruction or to democratize the area so that people will think that your intention is genuinely for the good of the people. So, then you even start convincing yourself of that, even though the real reason is for you to have more money.

Lately the answers to the critical questions about the war given by leaders running the war in Iraq are not really good – not really convincing. Even these leaders are naive and their being naive is causing a problem. If your excuse is to find weapons of mass destruction or to create democracy, that is one thing. But the war-creators know the real reason is for petrol money and Hussein is blocking the profits they could be making. Then they make the excuses as mentioned. Later, they actually convince themselves of these reasons, like the child who says they are sick so they don't have to study.

Robert: Some people see this and have the common sense to know that the excuses are "just that." So what can people do to change this?

Rinpoche: People in the US who know how to write well, or speak well, should use those abilities: to write books, etc., to reach out and encourage people to develop their common sense. Like I said, senior George Bush and junior George Bush both attacked Saddam Hussein. But the difference is what? You can analyze what they have done. What do thoughtful people do? What do unthoughtful people do? For example, junior George Bush is being misused by partners who want to make war in Iraq for their own purpose and to make money. But, junior George Bush is naive because he says his father told him to make war. Who is his father? It is not senior George Bush. It is another father; his father in the sky, who helped him with his alcoholism. Then he thinks that he has been ordered by this father to attack Iraq. He did say that. That is very naive. How can an elected president say such a thing? Oh, because he is elected by people and not by God.

Robert: That statement about God telling him to attack Iraq was quoted in the European papers. It was not in the American press.

Rinpoche: I see.

As I have told you, people who are trained at university to only believe what they can see are learning a wrong way of seeing the world. Similarly it is wrong if you can only react upon what you see.

Robert: If you look at the issues of sickness, poverty, and warfare, as mentioned in the Buddhist texts, which one of these do you think is the most significant or problematic right now?

Rinpoche: Sickness is just nature. Poverty... One should not judge too strongly about poverty or war. For example, positive war is needed as long as there is evil. If there is no evil, then there is no need for war. I am speaking about a wise, positive war, not a stupid, but positive war. So, senior George Bush's war was positive and wise. Junior George Bush's war is positive maybe, but also stupid.

Robert: So in these times, if you are looking at what people can do to change today's world situation...

Rinpoche: Common sense. Improve common sense.

Robert: You mean education?

Rinpoche: No, common sense. Education is already there. But we don't need more education that creates the machine mind. If people in the US develop more common sense, then this will be good because the US is the most powerful country in the world. In Buddhism, we teach to follow direct logical science and indirect logical science. Indirect logical science is invisible science to help one judge and get an accurate understanding. In Europe and the US, all there is is direct logical science. They do not have indirect logical science. They don't know that the indirect logical science is important.

Robert: In the time of Thomas Jefferson there was an appreciation for education which included agriculture and industry, but also the study of Aristotle and Plato and other philosophers to understand human nature. Today, in education, there is much emphasis on science and math – again your direct logical sciences. And, there is a belief that if you are going to learn about the invisible, you should learn it by studying religion, going to Bible school. This may encourage a development of ethics and morality. But in the mainstream of our education, what would you suggest is studied to understand the invisible logic?

Rinpoche: Maybe students can be encouraged to review the good things done by wise people; what they did to develop their far-sighted judgment. As it is now, if people in power only believe what they can see through direct logic, then people with a far-sighted view, who know indirect logic, can do very little. For instance, many years ago, I was told by Trinley Rinpoche's father that General de Gaulle of France, when he was president, made it so that the colonials from the French territories and colonies did not have the right to immigrate to France. He could see what was going on with the religious extremists in Algeria and knew that if they came to France freely, then they could do all kinds of bad things. So, de Gaulle had far-sighted vision.

Robert: So it might have seemed at the time that de Gaulle was being unfair and people protested, then...

Rinpoche: Yes, but he made that policy because he could see that far away into the future. Senior George Bush was like that. He left Saddam Hussein in place so he could block a war with extremist Islamic peoples. The US could not block this from happening. And, if a war like this happened, the US would have to kill everyone. A war of the extremists would have been bad for the world and you would have to do this. But, if you can block it for the time being, that is the thing to do. So, senior George Bush subdued Saddam Hussein's evil activities and let him be there to block it; that is wise judgment. This is not based on material judgment or making money. Very wise, very wise people.

Robert: Rinpoche, if you were to look at the 21st century, what is your vision of what the world will be like over the next 20, 30, or 40 years, based on how things are now?

Rinpoche: Later, if things continue as they are now, then there is much danger. Much bad will happen. People in the US can waste their time in researching such things as President Clinton's love affair with Monica Lewinski.

Robert: Focusing on the wrong thing.

Rinpoche: Yes, without using any common sense. People use all the time and energy and put all sorts of things in the paper about Clinton and Monica Lewinski. OK, that's enough. But they keep on and on, like a robot. If people are like this at the Pentagon, the military leaders, what will happen? If the people involved with foreign affairs are like that, what will happen? If the President and the men around him become like this, what will happen? Then things just go on like a robot, with no use of higher logic, no common sense. If in the government you have men like the one who made the inquiry into Clinton's love affair [Kenneth Starr] and published everything, if you have that kind of man in the White House with a lot of power, and in the different cabinet posts with their power, in the military with their power, if you have dozens like him in places of power then, OOH! You can make so many mistakes – men that are like machines.

Robert: Finally, Rinpoche, I want to talk with you about the environment. Last year, President Bill Clinton held a conference in New York about global warming. They talked about oil, the heating up of the planet, and such things as the growing frequency of hurricanes; the fact that within the next 70 years the earth's water could rise by two to three feet and displace over 30 million people. How should we look at these environmental problems? What would be a Buddhist perspective on how to take care of the planet?

Rinpoche: It seems that something like this is inevitable, but scientists can maybe discover many good ways to prevent it. Otherwise, Buddhists cannot say much because the cosmic world is samsara. You cannot change this world into paradise. Disasters created by the elements in this world – unless you are enlightened and the elements do not affect you – as long as you have physical form, the elements will affect you: earthquakes, the end of the dinosaurs because of a meteor, tsunamis; these things are inevitable.

Robert: In this country there are scientists with strong religious beliefs who do not believe in global warming. Then there are scientists who say global warming is already happening. It is a battle between two philosophies, not science.

Rinpoche: If there are any man-made causes to global warming and you can prevent it, then do it. Otherwise, if there is no way, OK, then you can exchange views or argue for fun. There is no need to fight about this aggressively. Just for fun or to get more knowledge, exchange of views is always good.

Robert: In closing, Rinpoche, are there any last words of encouragement you would like to offer people at this time?

Rinpoche: [Develop] wisdom. Wisdom is common sense. Common sense is judgment. People should become more thoughtful. Try to develop a far-sighted understanding through direct logical science and indirect logical science.

Robert: You may remember a Canadian *tulku* by the name of Namgyal Rinpoche.

Rinpoche: Yes, I knew him personally very well.

Robert: He said that he did not see society becoming

transformed or enlightened, but there would be small communities, which he called "pockets of light." He spoke about this robot type of mind and encouraged people to get together to develop their common sense. He did not expect such people to necessarily make big changes in society, but that it was important for the future that people come together and study and develop common sense. What is your opinion about that? In these times, Rinpoche, what are your thoughts on how people can remain strong with friends so that they don't lose faith?

Rinpoche: If you have wisdom and clear judgment, then important qualities and principles will not diminish. So long as a human has good principles and qualities, good, healthy friendships will naturally develop.

Robert: So people will naturally come together.

Rinpoche: Yes. Healthy friendships. These friendships will have lots of merit.

Robert: Good. Thank you Rinpoche.

Ven. Tarthang Tulku Rinpoche

ABOUT VEN. TARTHANG TULKU RINPOCHE

Born in Tibet in 1935, Tarthang Tulku received a traditional Buddhist education under the guidance of some of Tibet's greatest 20th-century masters. From 1959 until 1968 he lived and worked in India, accepting a research professorship at Sanskrit University and founding Dharma Mudranalaya printing press to preserve rare texts of the Nyingma school. In 1968 he arrived in America where he has resided ever since. Over the next six years he founded Tibetan Nyingma Meditation Center, Dharma Publishing and Press, Tibetan Aid Project, Nyingma Institute, Odiyan Center, and international Nyingma centers.

More recently, he has created the Yeshe De project, which has assembled over 755 atlas-sized Western volumes of Tibetan texts to restore monastery libraries and has distributed 350 different volumes of classical Mahayana texts, totaling over 2 million individual books, to over 3,000 dharma centers of all four schools in Asia; the Bodh Gaya

Monlam Chenmo World Peace Ceremony, which has been held 18 times since 1989 and attracts many thousands of practitioners every year for ten days of chanting and prayer; and the Light of Buddhadharma Foundation, together with a number of additional foundations dedicated to revitalizing dharma in both India and Tibet.

For nearly 40 years, Rinpoche's focus has been twofold: the preservation of sacred texts and art, and support for the sangha in Asia; and the creation of a home for the dharma in the West and the introduction of basic Buddhist views and practices to Westerners. He is the author of 22 books in English (translated into at least 16 languages), and the translator of several classic Buddhist texts, all available from Dharma Publishing.

I first became acquainted with Tarthang Tulku Rinpoche through his writings. In the mid-eighties I read *Time, Space, and Knowledge*. Later, when working as a drug treatment counselor, I read *Knowledge of Freedom: Time to Change*. What I was struck by was the fact that he was able to explain the most profound Buddhist concepts in everyday language. Since then, I have used and referred to Tarthang Rinpoche's teachings in classes and other books that I have written.

When I requested an interview with Rinpoche and was granted one, I did not know that Rinpoche had not granted an interview in close to 30 years. The method for this interview was different, for sure. I submitted the interview questions and Rinpoche sent back full, detailed answers, edited by his student Jack Petranker of Dharma Publishing, who I would like to thank. In editing the piece for Rinpoche, Jack informed me that in this interview, Rinpoche answered many of the questions his students had been wanting to ask him for years. Therefore, I feel honored and privileged to be able to share what Rinpoche has graciously offered to this volume.

THE INTERVIEW

(Answers: October 2006)

Robert: What are the root causes of sickness, poverty, and war? Which one poses the greatest danger to humanity in the 21st century?

TT Rinpoche: I am not sure there is any point to choosing between sickness and poverty and war. All three have always been part of our experience, all of them cause tremendous misery, and all of them can be related to similar causes. In some times and places one is more of a problem, while in other times and places another will be the source of the greatest suffering.

Because human beings have bodies, we must cope with disease. Thanks to advances in technology and medicine, we can now cure many diseases that once were fatal. At the same time, our lifespans have increased, pain can be largely controlled, and even chronic conditions can be managed. So the compassionate healers of our age deserve our thanks. Yet there is also a contrary tendency. The many changes in the world today are creating all kinds of imbalance, which lead to new forms of illness. Sometimes new diseases with no known cure seem to appear even more quickly than old diseases are conquered. Even when cures are available, we see case after case where the necessary medicines or treatment facilities cannot be made available to those who need them the most. So we are certainly not free of the terrible pain and sorrow that any serious disease brings in its wake.

The underlying difficulty in coping with disease has less to do with the state of our knowledge than with attitudes – our leaders' willingness to communicate, to pay attention, to take responsibility, to exercise compassion and conscience.

Much of the suffering that disease causes could be eliminated if the wise, the religious, and dedicated scientists had a greater opportunity to shape our society in compassionate ways. It does not have to be that difficult. The efforts you are making in collecting the material for this book are a good example of how actions that may be helpful to others in the long run are possible. Yet human beings are generally oriented more toward their own self-interest than toward the good of humanity. That is why disease remains such a fundamental problem.

Much the same holds true for poverty. The Buddha taught that the way to deal with poverty is to simplify your life, minimize your desires, and limit your needs. That is still good advice today, even if not many people are likely to follow it. If we could accept a less complicated lifestyle and share what we have with others – if we could change our attitude – poverty would not have to be such a problem. Wealthy nations, organizations, and individuals often waste so much that could be usefully shared with others!

Throughout history, many philosophers, rulers, and political regimes have tried to help the poor. Sometimes their efforts have borne fruit, but in the end poverty always returns. Why? Because we are not educated to share our possessions or to help others satisfy their needs, and we do not learn to be modest in the way we use the resources available to us.

The results of these attitudes are easy to see. In some parts of the world, large portions of the population live in constant need, suffering greatly. Even in the wealthiest countries there are pockets of poverty. Speaking in social terms, the root causes for this kind of poverty are not easy to address, so in many cases all we can do is offer our sympathy. Yet if we learned to be more aware of the circumstances of others, change might be possible. There have always been great humanitarian leaders, and today many people are dedicated to eradicating global poverty. Why not follow their example? After all, we have one great advantage: nowadays the global is becoming local, and a problem in one part of the world has impact everywhere. So it makes sense to educate the next generation to appreciate the circumstances in which human beings around the globe live, and to study how to bring poverty under control in every land.

As for war, its causes seem to be more fully under human control. Usually war arises as a result of territorial disputes, conflicting systems of belief, the struggle for power, or enmity rooted in ancient history. In other words, human attitudes create the conditions of war. If we could change those attitudes, we could do much to put an end to fighting.

Yet attitudes are not easy to change. When people are frustrated, they look around for someone to blame, and when people are dissatisfied, they may compensate by insisting that they alone possess the truth. If I hold one set of beliefs and you hold another, the possibility for conflict and fighting is always there. And when people with a history of fighting or conflict meet, the chance for real understanding is small. They immediately apply labels to each other, and on the basis of those labels, one side blames the other.

All these patterns are as old as human civilization. Today, however, they are especially dangerous, because we have at our disposal weapons with the potential to utterly annihilate our enemies. The more weapons one side in a dispute develops, the more the other side insists on building up its own arsenal. In the arms race that results, fear and anxiety are the only winners. We see more and more paranoia, and at the same time we see people holding on to their beliefs and convictions more rigidly than ever. Positions harden, and the threat of conflict increases.

As far as I can see, this tendency is on the increase. Anger and passion beget more anger and passion, fanning the flames of hatred, which at any moment may start burning out of control. It is easy enough to say that people should learn to cling less tightly to their demands for territory and their defining beliefs. But no one seems able to bring this kind of change about.

The way we live only encourages these trends. The media, advertising, and various forms of entertainment depend on stirring up agitation and excitement, which in turn encourage a free-floating emotionality. Like the high-pitched whine of a whistle, such feelings promote negativity. There are plenty of people ready to seize on that negativity for their own purposes, feeding lingering resentments and anger. Even if religious, political, ethnic, or other kinds of sectarian violence do not burst forth immediately, the seeds have been sown. Pessimism, nihilism, or a grim fascination with excitement, no matter what costs it imposes on others or ourselves, make it ever more likely that one group will come to see another as its enemy.

In cooler times, it may be possible to resist these tendencies. But once a critical point is reached, when the mind is already on fire, those who urge moderation or fairness or patience can no longer be heard. Excitement turns into hatred or greed, and before long the fighting has begun.

Our international leaders may speak in the name of truth and justice, but the side with the most power tends to take control of the situation. Upon reflection, we would all agree that as political fortunes rise and fall over time, who is "on top" in any situation is bound to change. But somehow in the midst of the struggle, there is little realization that any rise is bound to be followed by a fall. So everyone remains anxious to get to the top and not fall to the bottom. With more equanimity, with a more balanced view, our political regimes might have more longevity and stability, might be less flammable and prone to violence. But we human beings have not learned this yet. We derive our sense of security from power rather than from truth. Truth and understanding have little to do with these endless power struggles, and being right has little role to play.

Robert: How can we deal with these problems? What can we do to bring about positive change?

TT Rinpoche: The patterns that support disease, poverty, and war are deep-seated, and we cannot necessarily do much to change them. True, we can offer our prayers and try in our own way to be of help.

Furthermore, we can make changes in our own lives so that we learn to share more with others, are more modest in our need for resources, and relax our clinging to our own beliefs and possessions. And even if we do not have the wisdom to prevent war, we can encourage forms of education that promote mutual understanding and help individuals see how their own minds operate.

Once conflict starts, it may be too late for such measures. When people lose their families, their country, or their possessions, or when they feel that they have been treated unfairly, they naturally react strongly. At that point it may not do much good to ask them to respond with love or compassion. So we have to create the right conditions in advance.

Wise leaders and teachers have always encouraged all beings to love and care for one another. The Buddha, for example, is a living symbol of peace and compassion. Again and again he encouraged all human beings to take responsibility for their own actions and be aware of the consequences of what they do. Such individuals are active in the world today, and we can expect that they will continue to work for peace and human welfare.

So even if there are many negative signs, there will always be reason to hope. Perhaps we can learn from our own sorrows and tragedies how to deal more effectively with the destructive tendencies in our own minds. When individuals learn to make peace with themselves, their presence influences others. Perhaps in time the blessings of their actions and their good wishes will ripple out in all directions, bringing balance and calm to humanity.

In Buddhism we call the great masters who work throughout time and space for peace and understanding bodhisattvas. Such beings dedicate themselves to selfless action, and we can follow their example. Whatever the outer appearances, such positive attitudes are always at work in the world, and their power helps counteract the tendencies toward violence and make it easier to work against poverty, famine, disease, and all other sources of sorrow.

The real problem today may be that our leaders do not manifest these bodhisattva qualities of intelligence, compassion, and selflessness.

How many of our leaders are willing to take on other people's problems completely? How many are ready to take the other person's side? With so many negative forces at work, I can only hope that positive attitudes become stronger. But for that to happen, we need to investigate carefully what prevents them from arising.

As individuals, we must do what we can to help the forces of love and kindness spread to all corners of the world. We need to learn to understand others, to forgive those who harm us, and to reach out to those who need help. We need to communicate more effectively, connect with others, promote dialogue, and educate as many people as possible from all walks of life to turn away from selfish concerns. Of course, it is easier to offer such advice than act on it. It will take strong efforts and steady energy. We will need discipline and knowledge, and we must be ready to encourage one another.

In the face of the countless tasks it takes to make something of value happen, ideas about universal love quickly lose their power to sustain action. We may be tempted to give up. So we must prepare ourselves now, developing the understanding and motivation that can guide us when we run into difficulties. Only then will we be able to offer our help and communicate our support. Even then, we must be prepared for the possibility that as passions intensify, those who most need our help will be unwilling to accept it.

Western society has reached remarkable heights, yet no matter how many goods we accumulate, how many luxuries and technological marvels we have access to, not one of us can guarantee our own happiness. In the same way, even if we could eradicate poverty, disease, and war, new problems would certainly arise. The real key seems to be not to shy away from looking clearly and honestly at our circumstances, and at our own suffering and that of others. But that is just what is most difficult. The bodhisattva path requires a clear mind, deep understanding, and a good conscience. These are the foundations for loving kindness. It is a path we can all aim for.

Robert: What contributes to the problem of drug addiction and drug abuse?

TT Rinpoche: People seem to be drawn to drugs because they are dissatisfied or seeking excitement, or because their friends are doing it, or out of curiosity and the wish to experiment. The initial motivation is not that bad, because it is natural for the mind to be curious, to want to know. But then the experience leads to the desire for more of the same experiences, more of the same feelings. That is when the real addiction starts. The brain and senses get hooked into the drug experience, and the addict loses all independence. The desire for the drug takes over the body and mind, the senses and the intelligence.

Before someone becomes addicted, he or she does not usually realize what is about to happen to them, and they do not listen when friends offer counsel. But when the addiction kicks in, good advice from friends is not likely to have any impact. A strong flame of desire, of wanting, burns within the mind, consuming all other impulses and intentions. The addict is trapped. At least, that is my impression from situations I have heard about or seen myself.

Drug addiction seems to destroy any potential for the addict to develop positive qualities. There is nothing left in the world but the drug. Outwardly, addicts seem to be coping like other people, but inwardly they have lost control of their own humanity, like a country that turns over its territory to an invading army. The body, mind, spirit, and senses do not really function.

In this culture and at this time in history, severe drug addiction seems to be a problem mainly for young people. They may start off innocently, but once the addiction has taken over their lives, their opportunities for joy and accomplishment quickly fade away. That is the extreme case, but countless people live with similar patterns. Consider an alcoholic who can keep his or her drinking under control, or the person who is addicted to eating, or shopping, or gambling. Such people dedicate their lives to their addiction. In their own way, they are completely loyal. But nothing positive comes of this loyalty, because at the same time they have completely lost their freedom. Even death may not free them from this nightmare, because the addiction may carry over into the next life. The pain that results can hit parents especially hard, making them feel guilty for what has happened to their children.

The ways to deal with addiction mostly have to do with stopping it before it starts. Counseling and education are important. Good and trustworthy friends may have the best hope of influencing the potential addict through their advice and warnings. And of course, if people learn to relax their minds – for instance, through meditation – this may remove some of the nervous tension that leads people to crave new experiences.

In this culture, that kind of education is difficult. There seems to be a limit on how much schools and even parents are allowed to do to educate their children against drugs. Our commitment to democracy and freedom is understood to mean that everyone has a right to do whatever he or she thinks is right, even when a person's life is at stake, and even when the person being asked to decide is little more than a child. There is very little sense that young people should listen to those who know more. In fact, we may even doubt that there are others who really do know more, who understand the way the mind works and can pass on that knowledge to others.

As long as we do not receive any instruction in psychology, ethics, and the inner workings of the mind, it is not surprising that we stay hooked into the patterns of samsara, which underlie drug abuse and addiction. With no source of guidance, convinced that we know what it means to be free, we all take the attitude that "no one has the right to tell me what to do with my own life." We all are taught to trust our own feelings, without really understanding how those feelings arise. We never ask whether we are truly able to listen to what our own hearts are trying to tell us.

Addiction is in some sense only the extreme expression of this attitude. If I am addicted, I know what I want, and I will act based solely on that. Neither morality, truth, nor responsibility to others can stop me from doing what my body and brain tell me I have to do. Caught in my craving, I refuse to take responsibility for my actions, pointing to external circumstances to justify or explain what I am doing. With no sense of right and wrong, no sense of being supported, and little trust in others, "doing what I want" or what feels right may be the only source of guidance. Something similar happens at the global level, with countries addicted to wealth or power or any number of other things.

Once these patterns are in place, there seem to be very few antidotes. Criminal punishment for those who break the laws against drugs may have its justifications, but it seems powerless to discourage drug use in the first place. Education seems much more important, starting in early childhood. Parents, relatives, and teachers can all do their best, especially when the child lives in an environment where drug use is common. After all, we know that once the problem begins, it may be too late.

Robert: What developments do you foresee in the next 50 to 60 years? What inner resources do we need to develop to deal with them effectively?

TT Rinpoche: The patterns of samsara that the Buddha identified operate in all times and circumstances, so I do not expect that they will change dramatically. Some people today say that the apocalypse is at hand, or that the Buddha Maitreya will soon appear, or that the kingdom of Shambhala will soon enter history, and I cannot say that they are wrong. But my own sense is that the characteristic rhythms of samsara will continue. The world will not become a heavenly realm, nor will everything collapse into complete chaos.

One thing I notice is that the availability of space and sense of place seem to change in different periods of history. Thousands of years ago, groups of human beings were widely separated, and each tribe had enough territory without encroaching on any other tribe. At the same time, people were deeply in tune with their own land, an attunement that took the form of worshiping the forces of nature. This ancient shamanistic view of life fostered a relationship with the earth based on communication, respect, and balance. Today our world is crowded, and we have little sense of being connected to one place. The result is that our modern orientation is to control nature and to take advantage of everything we can, extracting resources and accumulating material wealth. Together with this approach comes the division of people and countries into the haves and have-nots, with all the strife that follows.

Another thing I notice is that time seems to be speeding up. We all have this experience every day. No matter how hard we work or how much success we enjoy, it never seems to be enough. There is always more to do, more pressure, and not enough time. It is as if the earth were spinning more rapidly on its axis. We see similar patterns in the cycles of competition and in the loss of a sense of personal peace. Whether the developments we experience are positive or negative, the dynamic that powers them is steadily getting quicker and more intense.

From this perspective, I would say that over the next few decades we will get more clear about some things and more confused about others; we will make rapid progress in some fields and stagnate in others. Some nations will rise to the top of the world order and others will sink down; some will compete successfully and others will experience hosts of new problems. In some parts of the world there will be more poverty, disease, and famine, while others will enjoy relative prosperity. In some parts of the globe efforts to establish peace will meet with success, but other regions will be unsettled, with frequent bloodshed. All these cycles may speed up, but in most other respects they will be like the cycles that every civilization has experienced throughout history.

One difference may be that nowadays we are more closely connected to one another, so that our collective karma is stronger. Media, technology, and economics all support globalization, so we can expect that our own destinies will be bound up with those of the rest of the world. This means more intimacy, but also more vulnerability. A change in one region or area will quickly be reflected in other changes elsewhere.

Perhaps this new interdependence will help us experience more directly the pain and suffering of others, making it harder to turn away from these uncomfortable realities and teaching us to care for one another. But it may also turn out differently. If we continue to emphasize our own individual desires – if we stay focused on our personal concerns – the resulting limits on our view and knowledge will be that much more likely to have a global impact. When feelings, reactions, and information are all shared in common almost instantly, it is difficult not to react without taking time to reflect. The result may be that whatever unforeseen negative consequences arise will spread quickly through the world, feeding on themselves. In that case, things could get worse more quickly than we expect, spiraling out of control.

Robert: Are we living in a dark age, as the texts say? How can we tell, and how should we respond?

TT Rinpoche: When people speak of a dark age, they are usually thinking in collective terms. But individuals can also live in the dark: lonely, afraid, trusting no one. That is a real tendency in our time. While we see globalization and interdependence on the large scale, on the smaller scale, individuals are actually more isolated. This seems linked to the fact that people are unwilling to share with each other: not property, not wealth, not education, territory, good fortune, joy, or happiness. Since everyone wants things his or her own way, we feel more and more isolated. This feeds on itself, because when you feel isolated, you cannot open up to others. Instead, you build inner and outer walls to keep others out.

Living within this darkness means living with little joy. Everything feels heavy and tense, and every action becomes an obligation. Your work, your family, your career all seem deeply serious. You feel very much alone, with no source of support and no one or nothing you can completely trust. The mind is not light; the body is not light. Opportunities for kindness and compassion or for welcoming others into your world are rare, because you worry that doing so will make you too vulnerable, or that your actions could be misunderstood or misinterpreted. Cut off from direct experience, you feel forced to rely on rational thinking for guidance. Because you experience yourself as isolated from others, you believe only in yourself and in the importance of your own feelings, identity, possessions, and territory.

Struggling to break out of this sense of isolation, many people desperately search for someone to love and share their lives with, but often they confuse love with sentimentality and attachment. At first they enter into new relationships with high hopes, but after a few failed experiments they may become more cynical and lonely than ever. Deeply frustrated, with no source of guidance, they can only torture themselves with blame or else desperately experiment with one solution after another, until they eventually give up hope and fall into a state of numbness. Not believing in anything, they focus on the most superficial parts of life, worrying more about how to dress than about how to live their lives. Blaming others for every difficulty, denying their own power to change their lives, they take on the painful role of suffering victim.

This sense of isolation has become ever more extreme. In the past and in other cultures, families were close-knit, but today family members tend to elevate personal interests and destinies above the interests of family. Because these patterns renew themselves from one generation to the next, we have little opportunity to change things in a positive direction or to educate the next generation differently. Movement comes only slowly, and it tends to be shaped by social and cultural forces over which we have little control. In Buddhist terms, this is simply the wheel of samsara spinning round. But if enough individuals feel this way, it may become accurate to speak of a dark age on the global level.

Today we see the consequences of these samsaric patterns

everywhere. With pollution, the world is literally darker and more hazy: in the cities, we cannot see the stars at night or the mountains in the distance. The weather is changing; vegetation is changing, and the nutritional value of our food is decreasing, perhaps leaving us open to new diseases. Hazardous substances are released into the environment, possibly without our knowledge. Focused on ourselves, we cannot see the global impact of our actions. Science is supposed to be our guide in these matters, but science makes no claim to omniscience. Some people look for prophecy in signs and portents and predictions; others rely on their own religious traditions for guidance. But the truth available for us all to see is how individuals are living their lives. How many people are really content? How many truly wise and compassionate leaders are active in the world? Where are the omniscient masters who could share their wisdom with the rest of us and help us foresee the consequences of our actions? Leaders like that seem to be in short supply.

Yet this is not the whole picture. Alongside the negativity and violence, the famine, disease, and poverty, there are many things to celebrate. There have been great advances in science, human rights and democracy have spread, new life-saving medicines are developed each year, and countless humanitarians dedicate themselves to actions on behalf of others. We should honor and appreciate such developments.

Nor is that all. Even if they do not show themselves openly, there are great masters – beings at a higher level than humans – at work in the world, sending the power of blessings in all directions. In Buddhism we call these beings buddhas and bodhisattvas, but all religious traditions agree that such blessings are available. That belief in itself may allow the blessings of inner peace to manifest more widely in the world.

If we can tune in to this level, we have the ability to make an impact. Whatever the external circumstances, we can bring more light, joy, and balance into our lives and the lives of others.

To do this, we have to change the focus in our lives. Today we look for peace and satisfaction in the external material world. We take refuge in money, possessions, and pleasure. We never consider that we could take refuge in deep appreciation for our human opportunities, in developing more knowledge of our own minds and bodies so that we can heal ourselves, and in sharing that growing understanding with others.

What we need is a kind of revolution, a turning back on ourselves. For all the blessings we enjoy, we know that something is missing. We yearn to free ourselves from tension, fear, and worries; we want to be masters of our own time; we wish for access to aesthetic and spiritual joy, and we long for unassailable inner peace. Even though we may be aware of these deep inner aims, we may fail to see that the choices that we ourselves have been making are not leading us in the direction we wish to go.

Such awareness is the first step. If we see what we are doing and where it leads, we can educate ourselves step by step. We can start with what is positive in our world, and building on that foundation we can turn away from what is negative. It is easy enough to dwell on the negative, but it seems more helpful to celebrate the dignity and potential possessed by each human being. We should admire one another and celebrate our remarkable collective accomplishments. This is the way to build the confidence that will empower us to pull out of the tailspin of negativity.

If we could start acting today, taking the first steps toward realizing our own highest aims, we would soon begin to feel the confidence and sense of worth that leads to deep and lasting joy. Why wait for someone else to rescue and uplift us? Why not act on our own, as individuals, in the name of goodness, dignity, freedom, or whatever we hold most dear. Why not educate ourselves, heal ourselves, and then share the best of the best with everyone?

In this world there are many views about what is best. Some think in terms of their religious convictions, while others have a political outlook, working for human rights. There is no real need for agreement. If we each work for what we think is best, sharing what we care about most with others, we can manifest in tangible, effective ways the meaning of our being alive in this time and place.

This could be called a grass-roots approach. If we follow it, then even if the Kali Yuga is headed our way, we may be able to prevent it from growing strong. Perhaps we can even reverse its momentum, transforming ignorance into wisdom. Though what we can do on our own may be small, or may not have an immediate effect, we should never give up, for each and every positive action has merit. Try your best to help others, to help those who need help. Do it your own way, and everyone will benefit. I do not believe that truth will fail.

Geshe Tenzin Wangyal Rinpoche

ABOUT GESHE TENZIN WANGYAL RINPOCHE

President of Ligmincha Institute, as well as its resident lama, Tenzin Wangyal Rinpoche is a master of the Dzogchen meditative tradition of Tibet. Since he was 13 years old he practiced Dzogchen with his masters from both the Bon and Buddhist schools: Lopon Sange Tenzin, Lopon Tenzin Namdak Rinpoche, and Geshe Yungdrug Namgyal. He completed an 11-year course of traditional studies in the Bon tradition at the Bonpo Monastic Center, Dolanji, Himachal Pradesh, India, whereupon he qualified for the doctorate degree of *geshe*. He is also an accomplished scholar in the Bonpo and the Buddhist textual traditions of philosophy, exegesis, and debating. Upon graduation in 1986, he was employed at the Library of Tibetan Works and Archives at Dharamsala, India. That same year he was appointed by H.H. Dalai Lama to be the representative of the Bon school to the assembly of deputies of the government in exile.

Tenzin Wangyal Rinpoche was the first to bring the precious Bon

Dzogchen teachings to the West in 1988, when he was invited by Chogyal Namkhai Norbu Rinpoche to Italy in order to teach at his center. He is one of the very few Bonpo masters living in the West who is trained in the Bon tradition and qualified to teach. Rinpoche is a well-known master, having traveled widely, giving teachings in Tibet and in the West for the past ten years. He is a scholar, having written several books and articles in Tibetan and English. During the 1991–2 academic year he was selected as a Rockefeller Fellow at Rice University in Houston, Texas. During this period he continued his research on early Bonpo Tantric deities and their relationship with Buddhist traditions in the early period of Buddhism in Tibet. Rice invited Rinpoche back to teach for the spring semester of 1993 and he was awarded a second Rockefeller Fellowship.

Tenzin Wangyal Rinpoche is the author of *Wonders of the Natural Mind*, in which he presents the view and practice of the Bon Dzogchen ("Great Perfection") teachings, and he was awarded a National Endowment for the Humanities grant for 1994–5 to conduct academic research on the logical and philosophical aspects of the Bon tradition. He appeared on the Discovery Channel in 1994, where he explained the principles involved in Tibetan dream practice as part of their three-part series entitled *The Power of Dreams*.

My first encounter with Geshe Tenzin Wangyal Rinpoche was by phone in 1996. At that time I was involved in writing for and helping to coordinate works of arts and events for the first purely Tibetan Buddhist art exhibit to be held in the United States in Albuquerque, New Mexico. Rinpoche cordially provided Bon Buddhist paintings for the display shrine in the exhibit.

I later read his *Tibetan Yogas of Dream and Sleep* and found the methods he offered very effective.

For years, many of the Tibetan Buddhist students in America were told that there was no connection between Bon and Buddhism. However, with the presence of such great masters as Tenzin Wangyal

Rinpoche we learned that Bon Buddhism was at least 15,000 years old and dated back to the time of the third historical Buddha, Kashyapa (Sakyamuni, the Buddha most of us have heard of is considered the fourth historical Buddha). In the mid-nineties, H.H. Dalai Lama recognized Bon as the fifth of the Tibetan Buddhist lineages.

To request an interview with Rinpoche for this book, I contacted his main center, the Ligmincha Institute, in the late spring of 2006. It was then that I learned that Rinpoche was to be in Berkeley, California in the late spring of 2006. I drove to meet him there early one morning at the home of one of his disciples. We sat at a kitchen table, had tea, and talked.

THE INTERVIEW

Robert: There are many issues I would like to get your views on, Rinpoche. One is the concern many have regarding fundamentalism, both in the East and in the West. On other fronts, we have this war in Iraq with many thinking that America will soon invade Iran. And there are environmental concerns and how we use and abuse our natural resources, such as oil.

TW Rinpoche: Let me start first with the issue of fundamentalism as you brought it up first.

Generally, some religions at their foundation seem to have more of a fundamentalist quality than others. When there is this quality, there is a tendency toward becoming sectarian; people become isolated and do not have much of a global sense. Even if they do have global awareness, it is in a very limited way, mostly communicating with their own missionaries. Outside of their own community, cooperation and dialogue are lacking. If you think about Christianity and Islam, there are groups within these religions who do a lot with openness in their communication with others. An example of this is the Benedictine Outreach program. In such cases, these groups even feel OK with some crossover with other traditions and will even do things like yoga or meditation. They are also willing to share, but nevertheless they are able to keep their identity as strong and clear as is possible. They are open to dialogue.

Fundamentalists have problems because of their isolationism. And they are growing and this can cause problems. How can you break this isolationism?

One thing you can do to help this situation is to be open to them. For example, we had some problems with the local community in Virginia. I thought, maybe this is a good thing that they are having a hard time with our presence amongst them. It is good to meet them, to understand them and to be understood.

I think that current American political thinking may be also contributing to this problem, creating more fundamentalists, supporting these attitudes in people, as well as terrorism. I think there is a way of thinking about religion as if it was like politics. Thinking about regime change. Look how Russia has changed and other parts of the world. In World War II, many things were changed politically. But I think that religion is far more complicated. Like when Condoleezza Rice talks about countries in Europe that are democratic, and which ones are not, in the last years. And this seems good. But now there is thought that now that we occupy Iraq, that it will change completely. But many fundamentalists there are not thinking about the political point of view. Sure, democracy may be better and it might be good if there were more freedom, but these are not the issues that are bothering them. They think that Westerners are challenging and hurting their beliefs. This they hate. They fear that the US is trying to destroy their beliefs. Those ideas are not changing. They are just getting stronger and they are teaching them to other generations.

Robert: So what I hear you saying, Rinpoche, is that it is one thing to cause change politically. For example, at one time there were more monarchies in Europe. Now there are more democracies and other forms of government. So, political structures may change, but it is another thing to change religious ideologies. And somehow – at this time – we have gotten the two mixed.

TW Rinpoche: Yes, exactly.

Robert: In that way, Rinpoche, I think that there are many in the Middle East that view this as a "resurrection," if you will, of the Middle Ages and the Crusades.

TW Rinpoche: I think that mixing these two issues [political structures and religious ideologies] is quite problematic. This is very difficult. People who have a strong sense of their fundamentalist view seem to be hurting the world today. Their point of view is dominating. Maybe, for example, there are a few Buddhist practitioners around who may be able to maintain their openness, but if others with these views are around and are not open, what can you do? You try to communicate and that does not work. The isolation is so strong.

Robert: What did you do at Ligmincha? You said you had to deal with the community around you?

TW Rinpoche: Basically, when we tried to move, we met resistance from some who said we were devil worshipers because they had seen images of our guardian and protector deities. They tried to spread the word around, and it got back to the people who we were trying to buy from. So I thought, "Well OK. They do not want to welcome us so maybe this is best that we don't move there." So we didn't and it made us think about how we were approaching the whole situation. We had originally gone through formal local government channels in looking for the place, and we decided that maybe we should just go to the people directly. I went out to the neighborhood, meeting and visiting with people. I introduced myself, said I was Tibetan. I told them what happened to my country; I explained what we believe; that we don't believe in violence. We try to protect nature, we try to be peaceful meditators. You know, we are just peaceful people. Do you have any problem if we move here? So you see, person to person. And people responded, thinking that, "You know, you have humor, personality, seem like you have a regular life." So, we made a personal connection rather than relying on some intermediary connection or other people. This was most powerful and in the end, people didn't have any problem with us.

Robert: So large organizations tend to be more politically conscious and they project what they think is going to be the problem. The higher they get the more confused they are, and really don't represent accurately what people need or want.

TW Rinpoche: In the high level of politics there are lots of stories. Not just one thing is involved in a situation; there are economic reasons, issues of national pride, there are personal issues, some fundamentalistic issues. Of course, people will say it is maybe one thing or another when in fact there are many reasons. Whatever we decide and whatever the reasons we do what we do, people need to begin to think of how this affects matters in the global sense, and humanity; are we doing something that is helping or damaging? If you think long term and not short term, people may learn to think differently. In the short term, immediate visions may just focus on winning an election so people think this way. That's not good. Of course you may need to focus in this way, but the long-term goals should be kept in mind. Whoever we elect should really believe in the long term or have an awareness of the long-term goals, regardless of the immediate political consequences. For people and history will always remember those who do not pay attention to the long term.

Robert: In Native American tradition this is like the principle of the seventh generation; to be mindful to consider how what you are doing may impact the environment and people for seven generations. This is more important than the immediate gratification of having everyone on your side and your team or interests winning.

TW Rinpoche: Absolutely.

Robert: In the mid-eighties, H.H. Dalai Lama, Ven. Kalu Rinpoche, and H.E. Jamgon Kongtrol Rinpoche offered the empowerment and teachings on the Kalachakra Tantra. In some of the talks during those events, they spoke of the coming of a dark age. Some said we were in the beginnings of a dark age. Others said we were about to enter into one. Where do you think we stand, Rinpoche? And do you think that the rising fundamentalism is an indicator?

TW Rinpoche: Let us say it this way: there may be different explanations about a dark age or a future dark age. From a strict Buddhist point of view, there may be some cosmological reference that points to a certain specific time. I am not that familiar with such a cosmology. But generally speaking, it is said that when the Buddha was actually alive and teaching on Earth, that this was a golden time. Over time, since his passing, times have diminished so that now, his teaching or speech [the dharma] is what has been most important. But now it seems that the teachings are getting more watered down or polluted. Maybe 50 to 100 years ago, people who practiced dharma were in a different situation and understanding, whereas today people use this and that [i.e. pick and choose based more on convenience] and things are getting more polluted. In that sense, one could speak of a dark age. But, going back to your original question about fundamentalism, I don't see this connected to a dark age. I don't even really see wars as an indicator either. Wars have happened throughout history; fundamentalism and wars waged in the name of religion have been going on throughout history.

For me a dark age has to be connected to something bigger than these. For me, the biggest indicator is family values. The values in the culture are more of a big threat in our current time. I see a lack of people having trust in business, having respect for elders, respect to parents, respect to families, the sense of connecting to families and taking care of each other. People need to feel a sense of responsibility: to my parents, my elders, my family, the place where I live. That they do not, I find scary. Sometimes I bring up these issues when I teach. People look at me [as if to say] "What are you talking about?" It's like, these issues are not even in their minds. For me, this is not a good sign. Some basic values, fundamental values of humans are being lost. I think that much of this has to do with what has evolved over time as the direction of Western culture.

Robert: A teacher that I studied with for years, Ven. Khenpo Karthar Rinpoche said that a dark age is an accumulation of negative impressions experienced collectively which can, of course, be things like wars and such. But what you are seeing as an important indicator are very basic things to human survival: how we take care of our families, how we take care of our children, how we take care of our elders. It appears we can worry about the global things all we like, but unless we take care of what and who is around us locally, we are in even more trouble.

TW Rinpoche: Yes. In terms of these basic qualities, I'll give you a specific example.

In the Bon tradition, there is the concept of Four Guests. Four Guests are enlightened beings, semi-enlightened beings, karmic guests such as family and friends immediately around us, and then there are "object of compassion guests" or people who are in need. If you look at yourself, you are supposed to have four relationships. These relationships are not necessarily equal or the same. Americans have this notion about democracy as being something like an equal-ness, as if everything is flat or on the same level. The truth is that this is never the case. For example, a president needs to follow the law, so the law is higher than the president. In society we have to accept some kind of hierarchy. In hierarchy, we are not speaking about a fundamentalist view or a dictatorship – such hierarchies are terrible – but there should be some kind of enlightened, harmonized hierarchy. This has to do with who we value. One cannot dictate this. It has to come from oneself.

That sense of valuing some relations from the standpoint of an enlightened hierarchy is missing. Native Americans would speak about their elders. In Tibetan culture, we also show respect towards our elders, you know, people who are older than us, more senior in the realization in their [dharma] practices, have achieved more in society. In our culture, we show respect and honor these elders. One sign of respect is to listen to them and follow [their advice], not to discuss and argue with them.

Then, there are those who are lower than you. Even if you think of yourself as needy, there are others who are more needy and can use your help. You need to find these people and help them.

When you have this perspective [about your elders and the needy], you are shaped in a better way. If you don't have this perspective, you are more aggressive, don't care for anybody, you don't have respect for others as your equal, which leads to wars if or when someone challenges. The solution to such conflicts is to respect, discuss, to share. Without this perspective the challenge is that we come from a sense of isolation and if, by chance, we think we are stronger, we attack. This all stems from a lack of basic fundamental values.

For example, in my own generation and in my own personal situation, my wife is 37 and she goes back to her mom's and spends six months there; giving her mother baths, every other day giving her a massage, making her food, taking her to the hospital if need be – just basically taking care of her mother. She does this with a sense of joy, respect, and love. She does this even though her relationship with her mother was difficult at times in the past. In this country what our parents did to us might be considered as "abuse." But in our culture, we don't even know the word "abuse" and we would never use this word in relation to our parents. This notion of "abuse" is not so strong in us [as it is here in the West]. So for us, our parents took care of us and they may have done some things that we did not like. We just wouldn't focus and elaborate on these things, go over and over them, talking about them with others, making these issues so strong and dark in our minds to the point that, for the rest of your life, you hate your parents. We just try to learn from these things, not do them ourselves and even though we are conscious about the things that they did, we still show respect to them and take care of them.

But here in the West, even with those who are the same generation as my wife and I, the way they look at their parents is terrifying to me. Terrifying. And then, from my perspective, even in just one generation on from those my age, I see how much has been lost as regards values; the kindness that has been lost, the connection that has been lost between parents and children. For me this is really shocking. We can talk about war, but for me there is something that is hidden as a cause behind war. Something has been lost and it is getting worse. Something that people don't understand even though they say they do is the importance of the connection to nature, to their family. They have lost this basic sense of connection. Maybe they get a glimpse of it in some situations, say with their boyfriend or girlfriend, but a sustained and deep connection to their community and family, this they have lost.

If I wanted to identify something as a sign of a dark age, these things I would say are the signs – disconnection with everything.

Robert: I wonder, Rinpoche, if we could also say there is an imbalanced approach in venerating all of the Four Guests. So, for example, some people are good at taking care of the needy, but they don't take care of their own karmic relationships with their family. There are some that spend all their time praying to enlightened beings, but they, again, don't attend to the needs of the people dearest to them. Somehow there has got to be a balance, a more mature outlook that honors all of the guests.

TW Rinpoche: Sure. There needs to be a fundamental quality that human beings honor these Four Guests. It's like a house. You have to have a foundation, you have to have walls, you have to have a roof. You cannot just have a foundation or only walls, or some sense of what protects the building from an engineering standpoint, or just a roof. To be a house, you need all of these things. Similarly, you need to be balanced in your approach as a human. On the contrary, you see people who have no respect or consideration for the first guest [i.e. enlightened beings or sense of divinity] and sometimes the second guest. They see nothing higher than themselves. They may be a good person, well liked in society. They do not have a sense of there being a higher power greater than themselves.

We can look at this even in an ordinary way with people who have national pride. For example, in America it is good to have a sense of pride, but when you hear someone say "We are the best," who likes that? No one likes that. If the Chinese said that, I would not like that. You may have that sense within yourself, but this is not helpful in communication when you hold this perspective and say it. If you say you are the most powerful and you really are the most powerful, then there would be no need to fight, to go to war. But there are powers and forces greater than one's own country or interests. In our own case in this country, there is a problem with how the rest of the world views America because of our policies and what we say about ourselves. It is better if the world has a positive opinion about us. Of course there will be some that will not like us. But we should strive to be liked by most and to do this, rather than claiming that we are the best, we should show more openness, more communication, more skillful means, more dialogue, and patience. These are all very important.

In the current situation with war in Iraq and the controversy around it; was it the right thing, was it the wrong thing? It seems that some deeply decided that they really wanted to go to war and they would use one reason, and when that would fall apart, they would find another reason. For some, it looks like that. We only get small bits of information, so it is really hard for us to judge. The truth of it all is really, really difficult.

Robert: It seems, Rinpoche, it seems like you are describing two extremes. On the one side you have the fundamentalist or sectarian viewpoint where it is my god, my viewpoint, my family, the people I care for, versus an attitude where there is a lack of respect for the Four Guests. Somewhere in between there is a balance in perspective. Is it education or other factors that contribute to there being more presence of these extremes? And what advice can you give to restore this balance, thus a sense of respect for the Four Guests?

TW Rinpoche: I think the way society is today makes it hard to find the balance. At a fundamental level there are bonds of love that have a physical and karmic basis that for some reason have been disrupted. In Tibetan culture, parents show a strong discipline. But I have seen on television that when such discipline is used here, children call the police and their parents are put in prison. I mean, this is incredible – and parents really don't know what to do. So, your child wants to watch TV for 24 hours and you let them do that. There is no sense of discipline. So, there are cases that one day the child goes to school and does not feel very good and the teachers and counselors encourage the children to say what is wrong. So the children say that they wanted to play and their parents did not treat them very well. Then suddenly social workers get involved. I mean, it is not always like this and there are very abusive parents.

But, in this culture, people are very good in digging into and magnifying negativities. In this culture, say you are with a friend and they ask you, "How are you?" and you say, "Fine." But then they say,

"No really, how are you?" and again you say, "Really, fine." But then they go on and on. And this kind of questioning, this vice [looking for the negative], is a part of Western media. For example, in the case of the girl that was lost in Aruba. All the time on this planet people get lost. Suddenly, the media turns its attention on a girl that gets lost in the Bahamas or in the forest somewhere. I'm not saying that we should not be concerned and have compassion, but the global attention, the whole country's attention on these specific cases is too much. The media could do something more beneficial like promote good works happening on the planet. What about making a movie that is attractive and appeals to people, and you come out with a warm heart and emotions that make you feel more kind towards others?

We have seeds for such. But how many of these seeds, these potentials, are covered by the darkness? We have to learn to bring these seeds out, that light out, and expand them, so that there is a physical transformation and a global transformation. I am not saying that this is easy. But this individualism that is encouraged in this society is a problem, where people are generally just worrying about themselves, where everything is about *me*, my needs, my issues.

Robert: Rinpoche, if I might switch tracks here, I'd like to focus on the environment and today's environmental concerns. In your book on elements, you speak about having a basic respect for the natural elements that are around us. In the specific matter of global warming, President Bill Clinton sponsored a conference where they talked about the fact that regardless of whether we can stop greenhouse gas emission in time or not, the oceans are going to rise within the next 70 years and displace several million people globally. Obviously there are certain things in nature that are cyclic, what the planet just does. But, I wanted to get your perspective on what we, as individuals and governments, should be thinking about and doing to deal with these realities.

TW Rinpoche: I think there needs to be more education, more information. How many even know that this conference actually happened? Of course, when you hear such information it can be a surprise. Let's take for example, you smoke and are not very well and you visit the doctor and hang out with people that are more health conscious. That exercise, whatever, by virtue of the people around, your attitudes and ways of thinking are shaken a little bit. But, if you hang out with the wrong people who say things like, "Well who cares? My grandmother smokes and she is 90 years old." I mean, there are people that think like that. And, just because their grandmother is 90 and smokes, doesn't mean that smoking hasn't affected her. So, being around the right people and receiving the right education and information encourages change.

But, getting back to global warming and other environmental issues, the information is there, but these issues are linked to business and income-producing factors; basically economics. I think that between the Republicans and Democrats, the Republicans ask, "Do we make a lot of money?" whilst the Democrats think, "Is this good for *us* or do we try to save the environment?" The priority creates the point of view.

Robert: Profit versus survival…

TW Rinpoche: Profit versus future survival in the global sense. If there was more communication. You know, from the Tibetan point of view, we are always amazed. I mean from our cultural point of view, we were raised in very different ways and we look at the toys that children have. We have a six-month-old baby right now, and people come over and give our baby all of these gifts and we ask, why do we need all of this? We don't really need. Does our baby need all of these things? I mean, he really likes this one thing, a little toy from Mexico that he can chew and makes little sounds, and it is safe and he loves it. But, there are all of these things and just because they exist and the market sells them… And I think about these people who spend all of their time thinking about what new toy they are going to invent.

I have this friend who lives in solitude and he says, "Do we really need these things?" It's almost a problem of having too much. It is not a problem of not having in the West. We have too much.

Robert: It's like an accumulation of garbage.

TW Rinpoche: Do you really feel that? My wife and I have begun to feel that way. Maybe for some people they don't feel that way and that it is good to accumulate more...

Robert: Or get rid of it to get newer stuff.

TW Rinpoche: Yes, newer stuff. In Tibet, people have such a profound respect for nature and spirits, and respect for parents. People would go out to nature to worship, to show respect. They also went into nature to find themselves and to find guidance for their lives. People would sit out in nature and reflect. They would speak to nature and felt as if they were in company with nature. They felt that nature protects them, not just in the sense of providing fruits and vegetables, but more the way one human being protects another human being. So people look to nature as divine, as spirit, as a healer, as their guardian, protector, providing them with what they need to survive. The first thing someone does on Tibetan New Year is to take food out to nature before one has food oneself.

Where is that attitude here? I am not speaking just about beliefs. People don't have to believe the way Tibetans do. They don't have to go to that extreme. But the ability to connect to nature is lost. In the West you spend so much money on creating parks. But how many people really enjoy them? This sense, this connection is lost.

Robert: On an individual level, Rinpoche, I think people can learn or re-learn that. But it seems that most people do not want to bother until they are pressed to do so. It seems that many who come to these teachings, this information, only do so when they are sick, when there is some disaster in their lives. It does seem that disaster still is the best teacher... [Rinpoche comments: Yes, yes.]

So I was just wondering, Rinpoche, over the next 50 to 60 years, considering the various warnings and events we are seeing in the world in general, do you see a reversal of the trend in a positive direction, or do you see us going down a very dark road in the direction of more disasters and hardships before we finally begin to wake up at a more global, collective level? What forces do you see at a social or political level that can help to turn these things around?

TW Rinpoche: These are very difficult questions. Somehow, until you face strong disasters it is difficult to learn to pay attention and to develop a more global view. Maybe we just need to go further down before we can turn back.

Robert: In alcoholism treatment they talk about the need of the alcoholic to hit bottom. In a similar way, the President speaks about America's addiction to oil. So maybe we have to hit bottom before we turn things around.

TW Rinpoche: Yes, but it is really difficult to say. You know, we grew up as refugees in a poor place. Our [living] conditions were very difficult. We did not have many opportunities so we had to use what we had very well. But here in the West, people have many things, many opportunities, but they misuse things. One of the bigger cultural shocks for me has been how much paper is consumed here. When I was about 30 years old, we had our first retreat here in the US. There were maybe 25 people. After one week I saw the pile of garbage that had been created. I was totally amazed. After one week! In India, there were over 100 monks living together, I never saw so much garbage in such a short period of time. So, I am amazed at how much people use. Having come from India and with very little, I am very conscious of these things. So, for example, if I am in a room with a light and I leave that room I turn it off. If you are not using something, why keep it on, just wasting energy? You point this out and people will say that this is true, but they just want to enjoy. So culturally there is acceptance of this bad habit.

Robert: But in this country, Rinpoche, time is money. So let's say you have an office building with 300 computers. If all of the computers are turned off for the night, then when people come in, everyone has to wait for the computers to come back on and that takes time. But, then again, there is all of that electricity.

TW Rinpoche: Yes. One time I was told that one of the Twin Towers consumed as much electricity in one day as the country of Nepal.

Robert: Another topic I would like your comments on, Rinpoche, is related to medicine and healthcare. In particular, I would like your thoughts on stem cell research and the morality of such. The issue seems to be around the strain of some cells which come from potentially viable eggs. Those of the conservative Christian right believe that, because these eggs could be potentially viable, humans are interfering with life. Yet, at the same time, the purpose of harvesting these cells is to see if they can be used to repair severe injuries, like the spinal injury of Christopher Reeve, or Alzheimer's.

TW Rinpoche: I don't know if this is a "Buddhist" point of view or my point of view, but if we can do something to make better or improve the health of beings, I don't see the problem. I mean, if it is against nature, then we shall soon find out anyway. Nature will work against us. In a more global way, for example, when we work against nature, when we do things to the earth, like dig it up for the purpose of making money without any regard for nature, then, from a Bon and Buddhist point of view, nature provokes us, with such things as hurricanes and tsunamis. These things can be looked at from two standpoints. From the view of a shaman, one could say that the nature spirits are angry and now they are retaliating. Or you can say, from a strictly elemental perspective without even thinking about the spirits, that because of the disharmony of the elements, the elements are provoking us. One way or the other it is the same problem. SARS and all of these things that are arising as sicknesses can be like this – to lose so many people in just a few months. The possibilities of these things happening like the plague that affected Europe. In such a short time. It is actually quite scary.

Robert: Rinpoche, are you describing things as you do in your book? For example, from a strictly mechanical point of view you can, because of your misuse or disregard for how things work together, cause disharmony. At another level, there can be a basic disrespect for life itself based on arrogance. Here is where we think we can do whatever we want. On that level, from a shamanic point of view, the spirits do not agree that we can do these things.

TW Rinpoche: That is correct. For people who discover something like the dharma [the teachings of the Buddha], they may come to realize that life is not about how much you have. What you have can be useful, but a deep sense of joy and balance you can discover within yourself. Through the dharma and reflecting on one's life, people realize they can simplify more, use less, take care of more in their life. You develop a sense of respect. You come to realize that there is more to life than just taking care of stuff. If people do not encounter such teachings, if people do not have the opportunity to develop respect for what is around them, everything they have defines who they are. And when they lose these things around them, they feel like they are losing themselves. They do not even know that this is a mistaken point of view. They feel trapped. It is nice to have things and be comfortable. But we shouldn't misuse. We need to develop a conscious awareness.

Some anthropologists have looked at some religions as being fear-based. But, you know, if fear stops you from destroying nature, maybe that is a good thing. It's like when we see a traffic cop and become fearful and we slow down. If a person doesn't have this fear, then that can be a problem. So some might think of spirits in the shaman's view as being extreme. The idea of a balance between the elements may seem more logical and acceptable. In either case we need to come to an understanding that when you act against nature, nature responds. If you are not aware of it or go against it, it will destroy you. That's clear.

Robert: I would like to bring up two issues before we finish today, Rinpoche. One issue is about population. Many people say that the population on this planet is way too big for the resources that we have. Other than losing lots of people to illness and calamities, what can we do to control the population on this planet?

TW Rinpoche: Somehow right now it seems that the population in the West is going down, right? And the population in the East is going up. So, China is the biggest populated country in the world. Right now the Chinese economy is growing very fast. We cannot see into the future, but perhaps this economy and its population growth will both slow down. It is absurd in a way that, like in Africa or India, people can have five kids and here people have everything and they think, "Oh I cannot afford to have children." So, it is all in the mind.

Robert: So it just balances itself out over time.

TW Rinpoche: Hopefully, there is some degree that it balances itself.

Robert: Yes, Rinpoche, I understand your point here, but there are all kind of debates right now about birth control, about abortion. Obviously there is the more indigenous view that you have a child when you have a child. But, at the same time, all cultures, it seems, have developed some ways in which they have interfered with pregnancy and birth in order to curb their populations.

TW Rinpoche: [laughing] Maybe people in the countries with rapidly growing populations should become monks and nuns... I mean Tibet is five times larger than Italy yet Italy's population is about five times larger than Tibet – maybe 6 or 7 million. Now inside Tibet there are maybe a million. Really, in this matter I don't know what to say. Nature has its own laws and within the laws of nature, even when we think we are breaking these laws, but still in the biggest sense we cannot break these laws for, in fact, nature breaks us. Many situations, like war and sickness, are ways in which populations are reduced.

Robert: Yes, nature breaks us. The other issue I was thinking about is the economy in America and the West in general. Right now there are some people with vast amounts of wealth. And the number of poor is growing while the people in the middle, what has been called the middle class, is shrinking. There is a big separation between rich and poor that is happening. What do you think are the biggest or most important factors contributing to poverty today?

TW Rinpoche: In a way, I think in America, yes, the rich are getting richer and the poor are getting poorer. But, nevertheless, I think America is not as bad as other countries. In the past there were slaves, now there are not. So, whilst the rich are very rich, compared to the rest of the world, even many of the poor here have air conditioning and heating. They even go to Starbucks.

But if we look globally, in countries in Africa and elsewhere, poverty is a big issue. I don't think there is any one big outside or controlling factor around the world contributing to or making this poverty. Rather, I think it is a lack of education inside these countries. There is a lack of awareness, of education, not understanding the resources available to them in their own countries and how to develop them. I mean, think of how in America there could be people who could come up with the idea of putting a city in the middle of a desert and make lots of money with gambling. Or selling hamburgers, the worst food on the planet, worldwide. I mean, Americans, if nothing else, are great in marketing. I mean, making hamburgers global is an amazing skill. It's so strange to see in India, where there is both a vegetarian and non-vegetarian cuisine, and yet young people want to go to hamburger places. These are the "in" places to go. It is very strange.

And these people in America who have so much money. I mean, what can you do with so much? Do you need more things? Maybe you can buy and fly a private jet, but in the end, what are you going to do? You still live in the same place when you come back.

Robert: Like wherever you go there you are.

TW Rinpoche: Yes, but you can also do some very good things, like start a foundation. The good thing about this country is that you can make so much money, then have the opportunity to do so much good with it. For example, the Rockefeller Foundation. I came to this country because of the Rockefeller Foundation. My own teacher went to England the first time because of the Rockefeller Foundation. Two people living in one small house in India have been supported by this Foundation. So it is amazing when someone with so much wealth has the desire to give back. I mean, there are all sorts of laws around foundations and maybe it would be good if, economically, the government could help the environment by helping to subsidize things like hybrid cars.

In the dharma, when we are looking at the world and all of the suffering, we say that the root is ignorance. But here [laughter] it seems to be about the money. The root is the dollars. So somehow, we should understand that if we use less there is a reward for that. It is not like we can borrow on credit. Furthermore, if the government wants to help the environment more, other than encouraging us to use less, they should invest in things that benefit the environment. The less you borrow the more you will get. In Tibetan we say if you don't owe, you are rich. Here it almost seems the opposite, that if you owe more you are rich. This seems to even be the view of big companies. It's like a reverse [to the Tibetan] view.

Robert: If you were to look over the next 100 years where do you see things going? And, what would you advise people to help them approach this future in a positive way?

TW Rinpoche: That is a hard question. [Long pause.] It is actually quite difficult to say. If you look at your main question about sickness, poverty, and warfare, I think that the main cause of sickness is the damage to the environment. And, as I said, it is not that we have ignorance about the environment. It's really about the money. Warfare is also connected to money. But at the core, the fundamental cause of all of these things are the root poisons [of ignorance, attachment, and aggression].

The foundation of sickness, poverty, and warfare is basically our human emotions. Many cannot handle their emotions because they do not have adequate spiritual tools. And there are even those who claim to have spiritual tools and misuse them, becoming more fundamentalist, more isolationist, attacking each other and making war in the name of love or religion. The way things are now, it just seems that we are not in a very good place; a very troubling place; in a global sense, a community sense, family sense, individual sense. Hopefully as things go farther down and get to a certain point where they cannot get worse, things have got to turn around. How long this will take and when that will be is hard to say. My hope is that this happens and things shift in a more positive direction.

At this time, I think collective prayers coming from the heart are very powerful. When groups around the globe make collective prayers, their prayers meet and are even more powerful. This is my hope.

Robert: Thank you very much, Rinpoche.

Geshe Michael Roach and Christie McNally

ABOUT MICHAEL ROACH

Geshe Michael Roach is the founder and spiritual director of Diamond Mountain. He was born in Los Angeles in 1952 and was raised in Phoenix, Arizona. As a student at Princeton University he concentrated his studies in religion and ancient Sanskrit and Russian language. He met his teacher, Khen Rinpoche Geshe Lobsang Tharchin, in 1972 in the US and studied very closely with him after that time. He was ordained as a Buddhist monk in 1983 and is entirely fluent in the spoken and written Tibetan language. After approximately 20 years of daily intensive study with Khen Rinpoche in New Jersey and at Sera Mey monastery in Southern India, Geshe Michael received the *geshe* degree in 1995 (akin to a doctorate of divinity). He has also studied extensively at Sera Mey with Geshe Thubten Rinchen, one of the great living scripture teachers.

Geshe Michael has also translated over 5,000 pages of Tibetan scriptures, which form the core of the Asian Classics Institute curriculum, as well as numerous unpublished ancient Sanskrit and Tibetan texts.

From 3 March 2000 until 6 June 2003, Geshe Michael took part in a three-year silent, solitary retreat. At intervals during the retreat, he taught six Quiet Retreat Teachings to hundreds of students who came to Diamond Mountain from around the world. At that time, he started to integrate the ancient Buddhist teachings from Tibet with the yoga lineages that were preserved in the Indian traditions, and is now teaching throughout the world about the value of reintegrating the classical scriptures and practices of yoga, as practiced in ancient India, back into the authentic world-view and practice of Buddhism.

ABOUT CHRISTIE McNALLY

The wife and consort of Geshe Michael, Christie has studied yoga extensively in Tibetan monasteries in the East as well as with some of the world's most renowned yoga teachers. Along with traveling and teaching with Geshe Michael, Christie is a textual expert and translator of Tibetan and Sanskrit for Diamond Mountain's Asian Classics Input Project. She has also completed a three-year retreat at Diamond Mountain.

In around 2004, a good friend recommended to me a book entitled *The Diamond Cutter* by Geshe Michael Roach. This American-born teacher was able to take the 20 years of teaching in Buddhist monasteries and bring it to life in the business world. It was exciting to read and when Michael Mann asked me to do interviews with Buddhist teachers, Geshe Michael was immediately on the list.

My interview with Geshe Michael and his wife, Christie McNally, happened on the day after the International Day of Peace, 22 September 2006. It had taken time to set up the interview through his Diamond Mountain University in Arizona. Using Skype to communicate, I was at home and he and Christie were, in fact, in New York City doing a photo shoot for a new book. He was on a deadline so we had to be quick, but, given the nature of his and her answers, the time available allowed for the interview to feel rich and complete.

THE INTERVIEW

Robert: One of the things discussed when the Kalachakra initiations were given by H.H. Dalai Lama, Jamgon Kongtrul Rinpoche and Kalu Rinpoche was this notion of a dark age. I would like to know what you define as a dark age and whether or not you define this time that we are living in as a dark age. If you think this is or is not a dark age, what signs do you see that would indicate one way or the other? Finally, in that context and if you do, indeed, see this as a dark age, what kind of attitude should we as humans take in order to work towards transforming it?

Geshe Michael: I have two comments. First, in the Abhidharma Kosha which is the Treasury of Higher Knowledge, the main text used in Theravadin countries like Sri Lanka and Thailand, composed by Vasubhandu in AD 350 and like the Buddhist encyclo-pedia of earlier days, one finds the doctrine at the end of the third chapter which talks about the creation of the world and the destruction of the world. According to that chapter we go through these huge cycles, many kalpas or millions of years. It defines a kalpa and describes the coming of the close days, and what would be the signs. They define this time as a period when the lifespan begins to shorten. We as humans were supposed to have lived for thousands of years previously but, due to communal bad karma, were engaging in war, harming other people, harming other beings and eating animals. As a result, each time we reincarnate our lives are shorter and shorter until eventually our lifespan is only about ten years old. So, when the average lifespan of a human on the planet is less than 100 years, then in terms of this classical definition, that would be considered a dark era. But, also in that context, we have probably been in a dark era for about 15,000 years.

But I have a different understanding that was shared with me by another lama. It is one of my favorite exchanges and I would like to describe it to you.

When we were in the monastery, we did not do physical yoga. Normally, you have to complete your *geshe* degree, which takes up to 20 to 25 years, before you are allowed to engage in deep tantric practices. And, when you finish your *geshe* training, then, generally in Tibet you were eligible to go to tantric college and the enrollment requirements are quite strict. But in Sera [a Tibetan Buddhist monastery established in India after the Tibetan Diaspora of 1959], what happened to us, after I finished my *geshe* degree and Christie and I were both there, we were taking some initiations and getting some training together. During that time, this lama began to teach yoga. We were sort of shocked because I had been in the monastery for 20 to 25 years and I had never seen anyone doing yoga. I thought they didn't do yoga. This lama said that yes, they did do yoga, but it is secret and you don't get to do it until later. So he taught us some asanas [postures]. Then we went back to New York and we were about to start our three-year retreat. Christie and I discussed doing some Indian yoga together, to have some exercise to do during the retreat. So we went to a yoga studio called Jivamukti run by two very great yoga teachers, David Life and Sharon Gannon – very famous in New York. [They are Sting's yoga lamas.] We went there and did private lessons because I was embarrassed as a *geshe* to be doing yoga in a Hindu place. Also, it was expensive. In the first half-hour we realized that he was doing the same yoga asanas that we had learned in Sera monastery. We were kind of shocked by this. Later we had a chance to speak with the lama from Sera about this. "Look, these highly secret yoga poses that you taught us at Sera, well they know about them in the West already," we said. He asked, "About how many people?" I said that we had read an article in the *Wall Street Journal* that said about 20 million – because many are the exact same poses.

We thought that he would have this thing that they have in Tibet called *Peh Kyu* which means professional jealousy. It's a very special word that basically means jealousy between spiritual teachers. But, in fact he began to tear up – he got all teary-eyed, so we asked, "What's going on?" He replied, "Do you know what that means? That means that those 20 million people are yogis from their past lives and that they have been reborn into a golden age. It is a sign that if large quantities of people are doing these practices as a regular part of their working day, then a golden age is here." And he started to cry.

I said to him, "Listen Geshe-la it's not like that. They just follow this way." And he laughed and said, "They don't know. They don't remember. That's no problem. They have been high yogis and have been unmarked [not recognized as such as in the Tibetan Tulku system] and they are beginning to remember. They are becoming unmasked. They are very close to high tantric practices. And that means that there is a very good possibility that these people could become enlightened in this lifetime." Tibetans call this *kalpa sangpo* or golden age. And he was so happy.

Sometimes, when you have a black eon or era on the outside, it might – as is taught in the teachings of Chakrasamvara – be a good time, fertile times for a golden era to be happening on the inside. When things get black on the outside it can be a fertile or golden era on the inside. I believe that and I believe that we are very much into a golden era. And maybe it is because of the efforts of many great lamas.

Robert: Ajahn Amaro from the Abhayagiri monastery commented that, according to Theravada, we entered into a dark age in 1956 and that in the first 100 years of such a time there was supposed to be something like a mini "golden age" where the possibility for enlightenment is very strong and then it drops off all at once.

Geshe Michael: Scripturally I don't think they would date it like that. The Theravadin root text says that any time a lifespan goes under 100 years, that is when a dark age begins.

Robert: You are amongst sangha and travel in fairly elite circles. And I live in one of the most beautiful communities on the West Coast. So, when you speak of a "golden age" how much does that translate into community at large and the world around us with respect to global events?

Geshe Michael: I think this is the emptiness of the era that we are in. And I think that Christie can best answer this. What I can add is that with respect to emptiness, one person might be experiencing a golden era whilst another experiences a dark era.

Christie McNally: It is very true that when Geshe Michael and I travel around the world, we always seem to meet the same kind of helpful people wherever we go. We do not actually have a home. We are in our university in Arizona for 3 five-week terms and do 2 two-month retreats in different locations. The rest of the time we are traveling, so we get an opportunity to see a lot of the world and a lot of different people in the world. Somehow, everywhere we go, everybody is so kind to us. And it's not just the dharma students. Just people off the street. They are very beautiful. And then we talk to someone else. So, right now we are in New York City, and someone will say to us, "God, I hate this city. Everyone is so rude to me. They always rip me off at the stores." But that is never our experience. That kind of brings to light the emptiness of the places where we go. Every person in this city of New York that we are in now is having a different experience. Everybody knows a different New York, because everyone has collected a different kind of karma and so they see a different city. So, there isn't a New York. There isn't one New York. New York doesn't exist, not the way we think it exists. And that is the emptiness of this city. There isn't one city. There is only every single person's different experience of this city. They are all projecting a different experience. So one person could be in a golden age and could be traveling like not touching the floor wherever they go, and another person could be experiencing a dark age, and it would be just as valid, because that is what they have created with their karma.

So, that is our experience. I tend to think that we, personally, are living in a very golden age, just from our personal experience. But, other people have a different karma.

Robert: No doubt, like many of those in the dharma community, especially in the Tibetan Buddhist community, you have met monks and nuns who have been incarcerated. And, through the power of their meditation practice, they have been able to endure, see things as they are, and come out with a relatively positive attitude. But let us say that you and Geshe Michael travel to Darfur. And, indeed, because of who you are, at the time you are with them, these people may feel happier and lighter in themselves. But then, when you leave, you are aware that probably in the middle of the night they will have to flee their homes in fear of being slaughtered. Knowing that this is what they may face once you leave, how would you advise them?

Christie McNally: That is a really good question. It has happened a lot, because we do travel so much, people ask us our opinions about the corruption in their government or the violence they see. It is very simple and we say the same thing every time: The violence that you see around you is coming from you. You created it. And it is really hard to say this to someone who has had a really traumatic experience. Like, there are some of our students who have experienced rape – for instance – and they come to us and we tell them, "You caused it. It's your fault." Saying this is hard at the time, but it's the truth and it's the only thing that is going to help them. It is the only thing that is going to allow them to change their world.

So, what we do is that we start talking about the small circle that the violence springs out from, like the little tiny violences that we do every day in our home and how to stop them; the violence we do to our spouse, to our children. These might not be big. They might not be anything that anyone would look down on you for, but such acts branch out and begin to disturb the outside world. Those tiny little reactions to the irritations you have with your significant other, they add up and build up to war in your country. All of those irritable reactions that you have in traffic – every single time you get irritated and angry is planting a seed in your mind to see violence in the world around you.

We teach people how to stop their anger, not by a band-aid method, like saying you should not get angry because it is not a nice thing to do, or you shouldn't get angry because people won't like you so much. No, you shouldn't get angry because of emptiness. The only way to stop creating violence in your world is to stop creating it in your own mind. The only way you will get it to stop is if you can control your own mind. That is the only thing we say about that and it is the ultimate truth.

Robert: This reminds me of a story a friend told me about a fellow therapist who had volunteered to go to Thailand after the tsunami of 2004. Working in a devastated village, he met a young woman who had just lost her son. Around her neck was a cross, which meant that foreign Christian missionaries had just been there as well. Knowing that the region was primarily Buddhist, he asked if the local monks had come by to visit her. She said that they did, but they were not very helpful. He enquired why, and she said that the monk she met said that all of this was an illusion. He then asked what the Christian missionaries had told her. She said that the Christian person said she would meet her son in heaven. So here we have a poorly delivered truth and an empathic, but questionable, promise which was much more appealing to her in a time of need when she needed to be comforted rather than confronted with the ultimate truth.

Christie McNally: I do think that, yes, what the monk said was a poorly delivered truth, and that there is a way to get to people, even in the pit of trauma, and tell them the truth and it would be a comfort to them – if you did it right.

Robert: Geshe Michael, many Buddhist dedication prayers end with the wish to see the ending to sickness, poverty, and warfare. These three conditions have been around for a very long time and at times, one has been more noted than the others – or at least historically recorded as such. From your perspective, which of these three stands out for you at this time or possibly for all time? And how does the significant one impact or contribute to the other two?

Geshe Michael: Let me get to this in a rather unusual way.

We just spent three months in China. We were briefly in India, but mostly in China, and we felt a bit awkward. The Tibetans are famous for not hating the Chinese, but there was always this undercurrent. I mean I don't think you could escape having some feelings if you escaped your country while it was under invasion, you know. And so there was always this subtle bad feeling about having 5,000 monasteries destroyed, and a subtle dislike of the Chinese no matter how hard you try. I grew up with that ever since I was 20 and I am now over 50.

At some point, traveling the globe, we decided that we could not make any more ethnic jokes or jabs at people, because we have been in almost every country and they are all the same. They are all kind to us. So, we felt that the last frontier for us was to go to China and see these "monsters" ourselves, and see if they were just normal people. So we went and we purposely went to a very remote area to rent a peasant's house. A president of a corporation in Shanghai flew us to this remote part of China to an ancient Buddhist holy site on a mountain. This man had been at this peasant's house for two months and so we stayed there and did one of our annual two-month retreats. We got to know the local people. We did not speak any Chinese and they spoke very little English. We spent time together and we had a chance to travel around China. There is this extraordinary prosperity that is taking over China. I know this because I used to be in business. I used to be in the diamond business and I did a lot of travel for that. I used to get flown to Bombay to the top ten jewelry factories and investigate them, because we would want to buy one. I have this skill of being able to judge the economy of an area.

China's economy is not just booming. It is deep, and there is some kind of extraordinary thing happening there economically which will change all of our lives. They just recently tried to buy one of America's oil companies and Congress stopped the deal. This is going to be the future.

We, as a country, have splurged on the world's oil supplies for the last 50 to 60 years. And I think the karma of that is that other countries now will be outbidding us for the oil supplies because they are in a position. China can do it. They can outbid us for open-market oil. And why are they so strong right now? I was reflecting on their attempt to create a society that was no longer poor, a socialist society. The communist revolution, in terms of violence, was a disaster. But, in terms of its intention, and its result in wanting to eliminate poverty and make everyone comfortable, they have succeeded. And so their motivation to eradicate poverty in their country has created – Christie and I believe – this economic boom and they will be the leading nation in this century.

We tend to pray for poverty, right. At the end of our *sadhanas* we say that we dedicate our *sadhana* to the eradication of poverty. But, especially in the tradition that I grew up in, it would be considered extremely unusual to go out and actually shop for someone. It's just not done in the Tibetan tradition. So you have this weird thing where you have this nation that tried to remove poverty by violent means, but whose motivation, which is the primary component in a karma, was to remove poverty of hundreds of millions of people – I think that motivation has created the prosperity of China right now. And they don't even realize it.

Why were we in Shanghai? Why were we in Hong Kong? We were in the Shanghai stock exchange to speak to the heads of the stock exchange. In Hong Kong our lectures were to the chairmen of the stock exchange. We were trying to communicate that the reason they are having economic success is their national interest in removing poverty in their country. We believe they are successful, but they do not know why they are successful. They don't understand that it is karmic. So we just go there and do all of these lectures telling them, "You are doing well because of what you have done in the past. You made a serious attempt to eradicate poverty in your country. You had a deep interest in your people."

In other countries, like America, we don't have such a deep interest in the welfare of all. And in the future I think we shall pay for that. There is a very famous line in the Yoga Sutra which is probably influenced by the Abidharma, which says [translated] "If you maintain a non-violent way of life consistently over years you will not experience violence in your presence in the world." That is the emptiness of violence. It is very beautiful. And if you maintain this as a person, or as a country, a non-violent policy, then, I mean when Christie and I travel around the world, people in cabs stop and get out and ask us if we want their cabs. It is unreal, because we are not perfect and we certainly have many faults, but because we are trying to help people, we have this weird experience in our lives of people constantly offering us places to stay, money, or just wanting to help us.

So, my belief is if – from the teachings of the Prajnaparamita, or "The Perfection of Wisdom," from the core of this teaching – you can educate a large number of people in a population to believe and to act on the idea of karma, that what they do determines their world. And so we concentrate on business people and politicians, people who could institute policies of non-violence as a cultural norm. Then this world would change. Then poverty, disease, and violence would not be in anyone's interest. And then these would be eradicated. And Christie and I believe that these will be eradicated. But it needs education – it needs the perfection of wisdom. It has to be done with intention and it has to be done by a person who has been trained to understand why it works. If someone teaches who does not have this training and certainty, such education cannot just come out of good will. It cannot survive tough times, it will break down. The Americans will get violent if they are pushed to a certain point. Unless you have a background in dharma, unless you understand that violence can only bring more violence... This is our life's work, the work of people like you with your book: to educate people, and then people will understand that violence is just not in their interest.

Robert: So, I hear you saying that poverty and the eradication of poverty and the upliftment of everyone has the potential to transform the circumstances that create and perpetuate the other two.

Geshe Michael: Our principle is this: everyone wants money. So when we go to a city, like Shanghai, we go to the stock exchange, we talk about using dharma to increase your own personal wealth. And then they learn the principles and then they expand their understanding to violence and health. We have to "cook" them with the money thing. The way we are presenting dharma – which is not the only way but one way that we think is helpful – we go for the economic thing first and it works. We attract people with that and then they apply it to dealing with violence and health.

Robert: It would seem that when things are going well in a culture and society, more than likely what is going on is the result of good intention and actions that help most of the people. Perhaps the "good times," so to speak, are not understood to be the result of these good intentions and actions. But, when a culture or society hits the skids, there is then the necessity, and perhaps the opportunity, to reintroduce in a conscious way those ethics, morals, or perspectives that made those good times possible. In some ways it's like taking the notion of karma and the benefit of being concerned for the welfare of others, and then teaching people that not only is it "good karma" for them, but it actually achieves what it is that they want to accomplish.

Geshe Michael: Right. We were speaking in Ireland one day and there was a very famous journalist there [the publicist for Bono]. We were talking about these things. He stood up and was rather agitated. And he said, "Are you proposing that what gets me from Galway to Dublin in my car is not petrol? That it is something else? Karma?" And we said, "Yes, that is exactly what we are saying. Some people will die in a car crash from Galway to Dublin. Some people will not have any money and others will drive them there for free."

Robert: The vehicle is not always the vehicle…

Geshe Michael: Yes. In other words, the conventional wisdom on the cause and effect of how the world works is mistaken. There is no connection at all between putting petrol in your car and getting to Dublin. There is no connection. If you are kind and helpful to travelers, you will get to Dublin. It's the weirdest thing. So, what the Buddha was saying in the Heart Sutra is that you cannot see anything, you cannot hear anything, nothing works, nothing exists – what it means is that all of the things we take to be cause and effect, all of the measures we take, have nothing to do with what is going on. It is mind-boggling, you see. Every action a person – a normal person – takes in their entire life is mistaken and irrelevant to what they want.

Robert: My goal is to see this book has soothing words and advice to as many people as is possible. It seems that these days, when people look at the news, or are caught up in the frenzy of their own lives, there is much panic. But in particular, Geshe-la, in some ways repeating the question that I asked Christie earlier, let us say that you were able to offer a final word to someone in a very dangerous situation. What would be your parting words to encourage them or to help them with their circumstances?

Geshe Michael: Think of other people. When you are afraid, or think of danger for you, stop thinking about yourself and worry about the other people around you. Suddenly, the danger will pass.

Ven. Ajahn Amaro

ABOUT VEN. AJAHN AMARO

Born in England in 1956, Ven. Amaro Bhikkhu received his B.S. in psychology and physiology from the University of London. Spiritual searching led him to Thailand, where he went to Wat Pah Nanachat, a Forest Tradition monastery established for Western disciples of Thai meditation master Ajahn Chah, who ordained him as a *bhikkhu* in 1979. He returned to England and joined Ajahn Sumedho at the newly established Chithurst Monastery. He resided for many years at the Amaravati Buddhist Centre north of London, making trips to California every year during the 1990s. Since June of 1996 he has lived at Abhayagiri Monastery. He has written an account of his 830-mile trek from Chithurst to Harnham Vihara called *Tudong – the Long Road North*, republished in the expanded book *Silent Rain*, now available for free distribution, and he edited *The Pilgrim Kamanita*, a Buddhist novel published in 1999. On 16 June 2005 Ajahn Amaro returned to Abhayagiri after spending one year on sabbatical, visiting Buddhist holy places in India, Nepal, and Bhutan.

A friend of mine who has a closer connection to the tradition of Theravadin Buddhism heard about this book project and recommended I contact the Venerable Ajahn Amaro. He is highly regarded in the Western Theravadin Buddhist community and is known for both his knowledge of Buddhist dharma and a commonsense approach to modern life.

I spoke with him by Skype phone from my home while he was in his monastery near the San Francisco Bay area in the summer of 2006. As he is English, I asked him if he knew the Theravadin monks in the United Kingdom. It so happens that he is a close friend to my wife's cousin, Ven. Gandasilo, who has been a monk for over 30 years. A small world.

THE INTERVIEW

Robert: How does the Theravadin tradition define a dark age and would you consider this period to be a "dark age" compared to other ages?

Ajahn Amaro: According to Theravadin cosmology, classically it states that the Buddha said that for the first 500 years after a Buddha it is considered a "fortunate era" in which there are many arhats and the dharma is well spread and understood. Then, for the next 1,000 years there are less enlightened beings and there is kind of integrity in the teachings, but the general level of morality is worsening and there are more misunderstandings of the teaching. Then the next 1,000 years, which takes us up to 2,500, that is the degenerate times, where far fewer arhats appear in the world and much more misunderstanding of the teachings and moral decline. After that time, for another 2,500 years, things slide down into an abyss. The period of 2,500 years after the time of the historical Buddha brings us to the year 1956 or '57, so we are just right on the cusp of what is called a dharma-ending age. By the time that

2,500 years has expired, the dharma teachings have been lost, remnants of the monastic community have disappeared and the teachings have been totally forgotten. Then that is when Maitreya Buddha, the next Buddha, appears in the world. That is the basic outline.

But there are also some prophecies, at least one that I have heard, saying, at that 2,500-year mark [i.e. 1956], for 100 years, there will be a brief flourishing of the Buddhadharma. There is kind of an upswing for 100 years, right at that midpoint [2006] where there are more enlightened beings and the teachings become much clearer, and there are more virtuous and noble spirits in the world, and then, at the end of those 100 years, things slide into the time of the abyss.

So, one can make of it what one will – where you can think that we are in that upswing or already in the major slide [in the time of decline]. But, from the Theravadin cosmological point of view, this is the beginning of the ending times. It should also be understood that this is cyclical. It's not like this is a terrible thing and things are going wrong, but it is a natural cycle whereby a fully enlightened Buddha comes into the world. There is a fortunate time where the beings have a high degree of understanding, the level of commitment to dharma practice is very high, and the beings born into that time are "karmically ripe," having come into being at the time of a Buddha or shortly thereafter and there is a natural ripening. It is also natural that after that, things begin to tail off and degenerate, things go into the abyss. Then there arises another Buddha and the whole thing starts rolling again. So it's not like there is one rising and one falling. It is a cyclical process of progress and degeneration and progress and degeneration.

Robert: Is the process cyclic or spiral-like? Is there an evolutionary trend in this 2,500 years or does it really come back to, if you will, ground zero – like starting all over again?

Ajahn Amaro: Well, the Theravadin view is that it is not so much a spiral; the idea that all beings are heading towards enlightenment is not

Theravadin viewpoint. It's more like, no, you go back to "ground zero" and then there is a big bang, universes come into being and expand to their limit. Then there is a crunch and during the crunch period there is no space or time, and all beings that there are carry on living in the high Brahma worlds free from fall and restriction. Then another big bang happens and another universe comes into being and it rolls on from there. So, in Theravada, you don't have that view that we are all *inevitably* heading towards enlightenment. In our teachings the Buddha is very clear about that. The idea that all beings will be enlightened eventually is a wrong view. It really depends what you do with your mind and your life during the time that you have the opportunity to choose. We can remain in ignorance for incredibly long lengths of time.

Robert: So, in terms of the time frame that you were first speaking of beginning at the time of the historical Buddha, Sakyamuni, 1956 is the start or edge of an abyss time period and therefore, in strict Theravadin cosmological terms, we are in that 100-year flourishing period.

Ajahn Amaro: Yes. In terms of us now being in 2006, we are halfway through that flourishing period.

Robert: After that what happens happens until the end of this particular cycle.

Ajahn Amaro: It is important to understand now that in that model, the idea is to make hay while the sun still shines. While we have these islands of opportunity, marvelous and miraculous changes can be wrought so that when the conditions do come together then the potential for what can come forth for the enlightenment of beings is extraordinarily high. It's kind of an opportunistic model if you like.

When we are in a dark age, when things are not conducive [to enlightenment] circumstances are quite fraught. When you bring up issues of sickness, poverty, and warfare, these point to times and conditions that are difficult. How do you handle things when there is not support? It's not as though such times are completely fruitless or impossible. But, we tend not to recognize when conditions come together, when there is perfect weather, the perfect spring comes and then the garden flourishes, the frost has melted, the rains have fallen, the blossoms are out and it all kicks off, and there is a time of great ripening.

Robert: Is there any discussion in the Theravadin school about this time of the abyss also being a time where we see faiths of very strong dogmatic views, i.e. fundamentalism, arising?

Ajahn Amaro: There is certainly, when you see in the Buddhist scriptures the description of what brings about these degenerate times, and a lot of it has to do with people clinging to views and a lack of morality, etc. My own thoughts on the causes of the current rise of fundamentalism in the Christian, Islamic, and Hindu worlds is globalization – where we are no longer able just to live in or within our own little town, little region, to exist as a kind of self-reliant, self-referential entity. Because of mass communication and mass media, people are exposed to different ways, different kinds of people, different lifestyles, different views. If you were in India on the Deccan desert plateau or living in the south of the United States in your Christian community 50 or 100 years ago, you didn't have to think about, nor were you exposed to, these other influences. You had your own little worlds and you were quite happy to carry along with it. Nowadays with globalized media, we are hyperconscious of what is going on around the world. In remote villages in India they watch comedies set in New York or *Baywatch*. Suddenly, in people's mind there is, "Oh, my goodness, there is this other culture and it's not like us and we have got to protect ourselves because this other is powerful, and it is there, and it is coming at us." So, there is closing in culturally and spiritually because of this global consciousness. We are being forced into recognizing ourselves as a global family and with that there is a vulnerability that makes people harden their borders, baton down their windows and reinforce themselves. They don't know what these others are up to and they feel threatened, unsettled by that presence. I am quite happy to be mistaken in this view, but it seems to me that fundamentalism – which may dress itself up with religious ideas from Christian, Muslim, or Hindu doctrinal beliefs – is much more of a tribalism than anything really having to do with religion. It's a tribal identity: "This is my team. This is what I belong to. We are the good ones. They are the others. They are dangerous. We don't want to surrender what is good, true, or right to this thing – these people who eat pigs or bow down to golden idols or do these particular things that I find heinous and offend my conditional eyes." Such a response is animalistic, instinctual, tribal – to hunt them down and bare your teeth and start growling to keep the others at bay. This attitude dresses itself up in all kinds of more polished or seemingly reasonable forms, but this all has to do with the primal instinct of self-preservation.

But, there is also a bright side to this globalization. In terms of the flowering of spiritual practice, this same globalization brings about the recognition of ourselves being a part of a global community. That same kind of coming together, our unity as a global family and recognizing ourselves as part of a sacred living system, that is the other side, the bright side of it. Many people refer to the effect that the *Apollo* photographs of the earth from space had upon the global consciousness. I think that that triggered – amongst many other influences – a global sense of unity and a spiritual awakening. It also triggered the instinctual response deep in the reptilian brain of "back off!"

Robert: This issue of tribe seems so important. It reminds me of the story where the Buddha says that sangha (i.e. community) is everything. We are social creatures by nature, and seemingly very tribal at that. In some ways I see this as a real modern dilemma, something I spoke to Tenzin Wangyal Rinpoche at length about. Here we are, for example, where I am 3,000 miles from my mother, and my wife is 6,000 miles from hers. Some of us have this amazing freedom to be anywhere we want, yet at the same time it seems that there is also a price to pay for this; we lose a sense of connection. It may be that we have escaped many of the "Bergman" dilemmas of small towns and enmeshed families, but suffer more from a sense of isolation as a result. On the one hand, there is the sense of being a global citizen, being more in tune with the global family, but at the same time spreading ourselves too thin and losing a connection that is possibly more intimate and fulfilling.

Ajahn Amaro: It is the age-old tussle between the urge for freedom – "I want to be free. I don't want to be confined by anything. I'm going to break out and do my own thing," in keeping with the influential books of the sixties like *The Glass Bead Game*, *The Catcher in The Rye*, *The Outsider*, the movie *Rebel Without a Cause* and so on, and the idea of being the loner, the free spirit – and the reality that when we do that we discover, boy, it is really lonely out here. We want to be free, but we also want to belong. We are in this conundrum. In that context, it is interesting that in the American sangha there are so many Jewish people; that the grandchildren of those who came to America from Russia, Slovinia, and Poland, after all the violence during the war and even in the earlier time of the pogroms, make up a huge number of the people in the Theravada/Vipassana world of American Buddhism. There are the Salzbergs, the Goldsteins, the Kornfelds, Levines, Millers, Halperts – good Jewish girls and boys. That intense longing for freedom and not wanting to be confined by the *shtetl* – that freedom is worth pursuing, but then the matter of what you lose when you cut loose from the family fold is very profound.

So, one of the things that people find when they develop a Buddhist practice is kind of a great resource and comfort in the sangha. That yes, there is this sense of community. The quote that you were actually searching for is where Ananda says to the Buddha, "It is my opinion that spiritual friendship (*kaliyanamita*) is half of the holy life," and the Buddha responds, "It is not half of the holy life. It is the whole of the holy life."

Even though the Buddha says that and it sounds as though he is saying that spiritual friendship is about having a close, human community, he then turns it around and asks, "What is *kaliyanamita* (spiritual friends)?" It's not just about having spiritual friends on a human level. But it is also having friendship with the spiritual; association with what is lovely or the beautiful – the realization of ultimate truth that enables us to live harmoniously with others and is the basis of communion, friendship, and spiritual friendship. The quality of freedom is, therefore, found internally, but is supported by a sense of belonging on the outside. So, if you get it right, if you do this successfully, what you find is that those qualities of affiliation and belonging, of association and the keeping of rules, sustaining commitments and so on, those lines, those borders in our world don't have any quality of confinement, they don't confine the inner freedom found within the heart or spirit. That's the ideal [laughs].

Robert: If you think of the Buddhist prayers which refer to the sufferings that result from sickness, poverty, and warfare, which of these three do you think has the most adverse effect at this particular time?

Ajahn Amaro: It was interesting to ponder that, having looked at the questionnaire you sent me. What I came to is that poverty and warfare were both at the top of the list and that sickness is almost an offshoot of poverty and also, to an extent, warfare being the offshoot of poverty as well. Poverty and war together are the major causes of concern. I think that the element of food resources and the access to fertile ground and water, the ability to feed your own community, that is, in some sense, a key element. If everyone in the world was able to have access to food supplies to sustain themselves to a reasonable degree that would have an immediate effect on supporting physical welfare and providing for medical needs, plus the fact that often the most common cause for war is competition for resources. Nowadays, warfare is not so much based on ideological causes like conflict between capitalist and communist powers, but rather because of religious affiliation or competition for resources.

As we see in the current situation between the US and Iraq, although it can be dressed up as a religious conflict, from the American side it is getting hold of the oil which seems to be the key piece to the whole process. It is the desire for access to massive resources of energy, to get those and own those resources seem to me to be the initiating process for that war. I'm not a politico, but I think that anyone who is not comatose could figure out that deposing Sadaam Hussein, and the weapons of mass destruction, was just a very thin front for an acquisition of resources. Oil is heavily, heavily tied up with economic and political power in the world. If those resources were equally shared, or if everyone had access to the resources that they needed, then that particular cause for war is removed.

Obviously these are very complicated issues, but if there is prosperity and everyone has their own share and, at the same time, if the spiritual teachings that people follow guide them to contentment and gratitude as noble qualities rather than position-taking or the desire to destroy the other, then the global situation would be radically different. Poverty and religious competition would be greatly diminished.

Robert: Ajahn, with respect to the Buddhist notion of the six realms of existence, I have wondered if there is not almost a pairing of these realms in some ways. For example it is said that the gods who live in pride, and a bloated sense of self, will fall into the realms of hell which is dominated by the claustrophobia of hatred which crushes in on one. Then, looking at the realm of titans and the hungry ghosts, it is as if both are suffering from impoverishment. In the hungry ghost realm they do not have what they need and are impoverished for what is out of reach, and hence are in a perpetual state of disappointment and need. Whilst in the titan realm of demigods, those beings have plenty, but also crave what they don't have and are also impoverished, and always want more. It just seems that what you are describing is that Poverty (with a capital 'P') comes from focusing on the world in a mentality of scarcity and the need for more, creating a battle between the haves and have-nots.

Ajahn Amaro: I wouldn't put it exactly this way. (And as a footnote, it is said that the gods usually fall to a lower realm because they do not spend time accumulating good karma in the deva realm. More than likely they fall to a human realm or a lower deva realm to start with.) But the point you make about the titans and the *asuras* [hungry ghosts] is very apt because those are instinctual and destructive responses to lack, either from greed – the greed of the titans wanting more, their sense of jealousy of the devas and wanting to have what the devas have and that what they have is never enough – or poverty with the hungry ghosts who don't have much and what tiny amount they do get is incapable of satisfying them. So, this way of characterizing poverty and warfare in the world is a really good way of figuring it, I would say.

Robert: In Theravadin teachings, has there been much discussion about the environmental and ecological aspects of what we are currently facing in terms of natural disasters, either from a cyclic standpoint, like the 2,500-year cycle you have been referring to, or an even longer cycle? Also, with respect to modern teachings, has there been any comment about mankind's contribution to the problems or even the solutions?

Ajahn Amaro: Certainly, the Buddha describes that when we cut down trees, the rain doesn't come, and when the rains don't come the crops don't grow, and when the crops don't grow then people have no food, and when people have no food, they begin to fight with their neighbors as they are competing for resources. That teaching was given by the Buddha to the people to encourage them to preserve the forest and to respect the natural environment. And so we have a very direct example of how the Buddha saw how these things are connected together.

In the teachings about the longer-term cycles, and certainly in the teachings about the cycle I mentioned earlier, it is said that in the early, fortunate period, there is a quality of abundance before things get more conflicting and stressful, and as social degeneration arises there is a degeneration of the environment as well. The Buddha saw those things as going hand in hand. The more the competition, jealousy, greed, then the world is more laid waste. And then, life is very difficult.

In one of the sutras, the Buddha describes a slightly different cosmological model where things degenerate and the lifespan gets shorter; moral conduct gets worse and worse to the point where, at its lowest point, even the word "morality" is forgotten. There is descent into a complete morass of immorality and an incredible degree of violence, profligacy, and dishonesty to such a disastrous point that there is what is called a "sword" interval – a mythological description of a time where no one trusts anyone, everyone is fighting everyone else, and the time is totally degenerate. That interval can only sustain itself for a very short while, before things turn around and those who survive kind of stagger out into the open and say, "Oh, I'm alive... and you are alive too." Out of the wreckage they start building up a quality of self-respect, morality, and trust. But, in those degenerate periods, the result of that kind of chaotic conduct is a great deal of environmental destruction, and the ability to survive in an environment that has been diminished affects everyone.

Robert: Have you ever heard of a contemporary teacher of Theravada talking about oil, its depletion, and significance?

Ajahn Amaro: Well, in Buddhist scripture you don't have any mention of oil as being a significant thing. But the topic of peak oil is certainly a common topic of conversation in our monastery. Some feel that peak oil has been reached already and that we have to seriously consider the possibility of a global culture not fueled by fossil fuel. These are important things to prepare for, and some of the mythological descriptions that you get in the sutras, where things have broken down and everyone is warring, compare with these days when the wars are going to be over oil and water.

I think in terms of the Theraveda world, there is a strong encouragement for people to be extremely sensitive to resources, to be ecologically aware. Several of the teachers out of the Theraveda tradition, like Joanna Macy and Christopher Titmuss, are vociferous in encouraging that – to be aware of how much fuel you are using, encourage the use of alternative energy, to ride a bicycle when you can, etc. – and being acutely aware of the products you use and what you are contributing as an individual because resources are becoming scarce. When the oil runs out, we get situations where the gas prices are going up, there are calls for commissions and enquiries and there is a growing tension and fear. I haven't heard of any fist fights at gas stations recently, but I know that they happened before.

The whole thing is extremely delicately balanced, and if the system shifts to a point where suddenly gas is not available or is out of the range of people's pockets, then the whole nature of life, certainly as we have known it in the USA, is going to change. Every product on shop shelves has been trucked across America. Things are very rarely consumed at their point of production. Our dependency on this extremely fragile commodity is extraordinarily high. And so, it comes up in dharma teachings occasionally to encourage people to be aware of the things that support our life and to not take anything for granted;

to develop the perfection or *paramita* of renunciation, not to give ourselves a bad time, but to recognize how dependent we are and be aware of what it is like when we don't have x, y, or z. Through renunciation, you are learning how to be robust in changing conditions. You learn to live without. And you recognize that when you don't have the things you are familiar with and you think you've got to have them, that you are not making your own well-beingness and are basing your own happiness on conditions that are completely outside of your own control. Also there is the need to recognize that, if things begin to get quite scarce and there is a major re-ordering of society, we need to be prepared for a lot of conflict, stress, and violence. That is what is going to happen because people are going to be angry as they lack things that they are used to, feeling that they have a right to these things that are being being taken away or are not available.

Robert: Are there any dharma texts or teachings that bear any similarity to the Western notion of Gaia? Other than the interconnectedness of all life – that the earth is a living being?

Ajahn Amaro: Not exactly. There are references that talk about the relatedness of living things and dependence on each other, feeding each other, providing for each other in different ways, but not talking about the whole planet. Subuthi did talk about the planet as a single object but not exactly in terms of the whole planet as a living entity. What you have in Buddhist cosmology are deities like the four guardian kings or *lokapalas*, who are the world's protectors and then also, the most significant character that I mention most often has to do with the story of the Buddha's enlightenment. In this story he speaks of when he had defeated Mara, and Mara, in retreat, said to the Buddha [to the effect…], "Who do you think you are? You claim to be fully enlightened, but you ran out on your wife and child. You couldn't even hack it as an ascetic, giving up on your asceticism and eating ordinary food. You are a failure. You're no enlightened being. I am the one who can claim to be Lord of the World. I belong on the *vajra* seat." Mara turns around to his army and says to them, "Isn't that the case? I should be Lord of the World, not this failed yogi." And of course his army yells, "Yes, indeed! Lord Mara should be King of the World." Then, Mara turns back to the Buddha and says, "So, who do you have who can back your claim?" And the Buddha reaches down and touches the earth. It is the earth goddess, Toranee, who he has invoked who comes forth and says, "This is my true son. He is the only one who has the right to sit at the immoveable spot and claim the *vajra* seat." And she released a flood of water from her hair and all of Mara's armies were washed away. Then they all come back bearing flowers and gifts to be forgiven and so on.

Mythologically, it is significant that the Buddha has to call the earth goddess forth in order to ratify his enlightenment. But what that means is that the Buddha was fully enlightened but so long as it was just an internal realization, he was free, and that was just a kind of subjective state. Touching the earth, calling the earth goddess to witness, was an indication of his awareness that he could not dispel Mara without the help of the earth goddess. He recognized that, yes, there is total, unutterable freedom and peace and clarity, but there is still this body which breathes and eats and walks and feels the force of gravity that exists in the world. Even though there is this limitless, timeless freedom in that transcendent reality, there is also this material world, this body, this breath, this family karma, this life on the Indian subcontinent that exists – this has its own reality. By acknowledging the earth, by touching the earth he is saying yes, there is this element as well and I am not trying to deny or discard it so that there is some kind of freedom that is a rebellion against it. The freedom is so complete that how could any material conditions or form whatsoever inhibit that fundamental or intrinsic freedom of the heart? And so, touching the earth and recognizing his limitations, yes he comes from a particular family, yes, he has a body, needs to eat and breathe. That calls forth the response from the earth goddess and that is actually what dispels Mara and makes him powerless. The Buddha is not fully liberated, not fully able to dispel

Mara until there is that acknowledgement of our worldly condition.

What that means – at least to me – is if we are looking for freedom, then we have to include our physicality, our relationship to the earth, our body, our minds, the resources that we use, and our relationship with other beings in this material world. If we try to find a freedom that tries to ignore, override, or dismiss that by assuming or saying that it is just the conditioned world, it doesn't matter, it is just the world of form – pheh! – there is no significance in it, then our enlightenment cannot be complete, because in a way we are saying that there is something about it that would inhibit our freedom. Touching of the earth is such a powerful symbol – almost the majority of Buddha images that we see in the world are of the Buddha touching the earth – it is saying yes, there is this transcendent reality but, yes, it is in this material world, and the two certainly interpenetrate. When there is this full realization of truth, then the natural response is to be gentle, to live simply, to be honest, to live lightly on the planet and respectfully with other beings and to take enough to feed the body, but not too much or too little; to be straightforward, gentle in our relationships with others and not be demanding or run away. It is indicating an extraordinary balanced quality relationship to each other and the planet. So that in terms of an ecological teaching, I find that invoking of the earth mother at the key moment of the Buddha's life, at the beginning of his ministry if you like, is an enormously potent symbol that addresses that quality of the relationship between our spirituality and the physical and social world.

Robert: It also reminded me that although enlightenment is often spoken of in impersonal terms, there is that sense of responsibility or that ability to respond in the world.

Ajahn Amaro: Yes, it is not only responsibility, but also *responsivity*. There is a way in which our life is a resonance of the planet, and to live harmoniously is to cultivate those responses that are harmonious.

Robert: If you were to look at different levels of responsibility, from the personal to the collective, for some of the conditions that we are currently facing in the world, where do you see the role of governments? Can you see examples where they are demonstrating some degree of collective responsibility, or not? Do you think governments can be effective in contributing something to help take things in a different direction?

Ajahn Amaro: Oh, I think so. Just recently in Canada, in Toronto, they had a multinational get-together around the issue of governmental forms and invited the Bhutanese government. Obviously Bhutan is not without its own internal difficulties, but they have established this concept of "gross national happiness." A number of major world powers, academics, and politicos wanted to know about this and how it works. So here you have this tiny Buddhist kingdom, wedged between India and China – humongous powers to the north and south – with very little of their own natural resources and they have managed to maintain a quality of independence.

I have traveled there myself and there is an extraordinary degree of social health and general well-being as far as I could see, in a country that has a population smaller than the city of San Francisco, a human population of about 700,000. So, here you have one tiny kingdom with no political power at all, whose army is only about 4,000 people. I mean, with India to the south and China to the north, why bother; have a few guys for a parade and that's about it. But as an example, they can influence these major powers – the Canadians, the British, the French, the Americans, the Italians, the Brazilians and others – who were there at the conference, all asking: "What is this?" "Tell us how this works," or "That's interesting." And they go back to their own countries and they may be a small voice in the wilderness in their own country's committee meetings but there are those voices and they can chip away and have a major influence.

Or there are people like Bill Clinton and Al Gore who are speaking very steadily and clearly and firmly about climate change, saying that this is happening, be aware of this. They are putting their powerful names behind these causes to say, "Look, this makes a difference. You make a difference. This is what is happening. Look at it." These are influential people, an ex-president and ex-vice president. They know they have big names. They know they are listened to. So, what do they talk about? They talk about these major concerns for the welfare of the planet.

So I have sense of trepidation from the human capacity for violence and confusion, but I also have a lot of optimism and hope for the human capacities of common sense, seeing reason and the urge to survive and to help; those are powerful instincts. The violence and position-taking, the suicide bombs and the rampant statements of random fundamentalist Christians – these grab the headlines; like when one of them calls for the assassination of another head of state because of their political views, or whatever.

But when these leaders like Al Gore talk about climate change, this doesn't grab the headlines (you know, "yawn..."). Or another ordinary day in Bhutan with people cultivating their faith in "gross national happiness" and having committee meetings that make welfare of the public the priority over immediate profits. This does not grab the headlines.

But these things slowly chip away and feed that commonsense, basic, helpful, nurturing instinct that we have. How do we survive? How do we help each other? What does the family need? What does the village need? What does the tribe need? Those kind of changes are quieter. They are not so attention-grabbing. But, like water seeping through the rocks, such actions act quietly. Just like water, the seeping can open up some major cracks as it works its way through the system, and can have profound effects in its own way.

Robert: I guess in the issue of Bhutan it was relatively isolated to start with, but there were also some forward-thinking individuals from Bhutan that went out into the world and probably looked around and said, "I don't think we want to go that way…"

Ajahn Amaro: Yes, they did this quite deliberately. They made a policy of studying what other similar nations had done, learning from the mistakes of others and copying the well-learned good lessons of others.

Robert: I think what you have now is about $500 a day just to visit and stay in Bhutan. They certainly make it hard (at least expensive) to stay, and try to keep their culture intact, as much as possible, from the onslaught of modernity. Yet they also try to bring their people some of its benefits. But, when you are looking at much larger countries, like, for example, the US, the situation is different. You look at the model of Bhutan and can see they have been able to contain themselves. Then look at the situation with these larger, less homogeneous and certainly multicultural nations, and you might ask, "How do you get stuffed back into the box?" Certainly the reality of being small and relatively homogeneous is not the reality of such countries.

So what do you do to cultivate such notions as "gross national happiness"? How does a country – a government – say to itself, say to its people, say to the world, "Sorry, we have been going in the wrong direction and we need to change course"? I really wonder, other than nature's model of composting things that don't work over time, if there is any way of pulling back. Other than people like Al Gore and Bill Clinton speaking out, do you see any positive signs within society that there is a recognition of the current dilemmas, like global warming, etc.?

Ajahn Amaro: There are many positive indications. I mean, going back does not work. But we can go forward in many different directions.

Consider if something like the concept of "gross national happiness" was being talked about in some respectful way rather than being made fun of, and questions of what actually contributes to people's welfare, what makes us more complete as a family, as a society, what is the source of real well-being? When powerful voices begin to talk about these things, they are bringing in ideas and directions that are part of the solution rather than hanging on the problem, or ignoring the problem.

To me, there are many influences that are extremely beneficial. Most of them are grass-roots elements of people pulling their lives together, improving their own living situations; local programs for developing education, projects to improve the welfare of people locally that, again, don't grab the headlines. There are many elements whereby those kind of wholesome and ingenious aspects of society are being carried out. They don't get a lot of attention, they are not made much of because war and entertainment grab the attention and so much of it blurs the surfaces that the shelves of Wal-Mart are kept stocked (from China) and keep *American Idol* and reality TV running so that the masses will stay distracted. I can understand that – it is very much a part of the "decline and fall of the empire" model.

But, I certainly see that along with things falling apart, there is, again, this common sense and our own human yearning that says, "We can do better than this. We don't have to go along with this." Often the overt degeneration, crassness and coarseness just pushes people to say, "I'm just not going to go along with this. I'm going to do something different. This is a status quo that I just can't go along with." The kind of awfulness of it can actually produce its opposite, and that is one of the ways that nature works in that things always create their opposite. It is not simply that things are hyper-materialistic and lost in a cycle of greed. In our monastery, there are those who come here as good-hearted and have decided that they can't go along with the mainstream values, that they want to do something more radical with their lives. They see that the development of their spirituality is the only way to really bring benefit and it is the best thing they can do with their lives.

If things are not so extreme or degenerate on the external level, you don't feel pushed to ask questions of yourself, such as "What is of value? What is important? What do I really want to do with my life?" If the status quo is a bit more moderate, you are more able to bumble along and make do with it. It is just when things get to a point of offensiveness and these people say, "Hey I'm out. I'm not going to play with this." So here we see that kind of effect on one's inner resolution and intuition.

There is a lot of grass-roots environmental and political change; thousands of groups, like that organization, MoveOn.org that was started by four people in a house in Berkeley with a lot of connections and some skillful technical support. A tiny group of people moving mountains, just because they see a need, because they say, "I'm not going to go along with it [the status quo]. How can we do this skillfully?" Or someone like Julia Butterfly, just one preacher's daughter who climbs up a tree, and nowadays she goes nonstop as a spokesperson for the environmental protection movement.

Those kind of influences, where they are well placed, well thought-out, heartful, and non-contentious – they are like the groundwater seeping through the rocks. There is a tremendous amount of that kind of activity. And it's not just the white middle-class community either. It's also within the black community, the Hispanic community – you have these kind of quiet, powerful integrative presences in the culture which are slowly, gently beavering away, providing the alternative – being part of the solution.

Robert: If this book were to go to very troubled areas of the world, what kind of wisdom or words of encouragement would you give to people in dire and dangerous circumstances who can't necessarily cultivate much of a spiritual-centered life? For example, if someone lives on a street where there are car bombs going off, what would you say to them?

Ajahn Amaro: The things that really help are universal human qualities. These don't necessarily rely on Buddhism or dharma centers. I would encourage qualities like moral integrity: in the case of a bomb going off in your street, you are determined that you are not going to get caught up in anger or revenge. You are not going to respond with hatred or a kind of reactivity. I would encourage people to take a vow of non-contention. This doesn't mean doing nothing. But rather, not seeing people as separate, getting caught up in a cycle of hatred, anger, and self-righteous indignation. I would encourage people to be committed to practicing honesty, straightforwardness, and non-contention.

That may sound wooly and airy-fairy, but it is a really important thing. If you are face to face with a person whose family has just been blown up, or they have experienced some other terrible loss, their immediate reaction is vengefulness, or hatred, or intense aversion. If you are committed to non-contention, to non-violence, to that kind of moral integrity, you are going to be straight with them, you are going to encourage them toward non-hatred, not that they are going to like what is happening to them. Point out that it is not helpful to harbor ill will towards even those people who have acted so destructively towards them. We do not have to like what they have done, but we don't have to hate them for it. That is an incredibly valuable thing; an extraordinarily powerful glue that holds us together, and it is certainly my experience of Buddhist practice.

It is a crucial thing for anyone to learn, that loving kindness does not mean we are trying to like everything and to love those who have just blown your family up. But, what you can do is to refuse to hate them. Just like in the book of Ettie Hillesum, a Dutch woman who was sent off to Auschwitz. The letters and diary entries in this book are quite remarkable. She was in Holland and she utterly refused to hate the Nazis because she saw that that was going to poison her above everything else. So she had this insight that she was not going to dwell in hatred and aversion towards these people who were so utterly destructive and despicable, destroying her culture and her family. Even on the cattle trucks on the way to Auschwitz, she still held to this, not in a kind of airy-fairy way, she was just resolute in not dwelling in hatred and cultivating compassion for the derangement of the people who did this to them. They say she was actually singing as the cattle truck pulled out, and that her last message was a postcard, chucked out of the air vent of the cattle truck and found by a local farmer. Even then, on this postcard, she was refusing to hate the people who were taking her to her own destruction. So that is a powerful force that we can cultivate.

Similarly, there is that universal quality of generosity; that basic quality of being ready to have time for each other, to share what we have.

So these elements, generosity and moral integrity, are the two things that are universally powerful and beneficial whatever situation we are in. Even if we are in the most degraded and difficult circumstances, we can still act in these ways. Another example is Lama Palden Gyatso, the lama who had been imprisoned by the Chinese for 27 years. He refused to hate the Chinese. He would not hate his torturers and that gave him power over them in a way. They could not break him. Or look at the novel, *One Day in the Life of Ivan Denisovich*, where you break the system by acting in a manner that says, "I am not going to be subdued by you. I am not going to play your game. But I won't play your game by resisting you either." Find that place in the heart that can be compassionate, this quiet and powerful force, and remember that we do have these abilities. It's always up to us to choose if we dwell in hatred and aversion or whether we expand the heart to encompass.

In the "Simile of the Saw," the example the Buddha gave was, even if a person were captured by robbers and their limbs were being sawed from their body with a two-handled saw, if that person were to give rise to a thought of hatred towards those people, they would not be practicing his teachings. Rather they should think, "May they be happy, may they be free of suffering, may they be at ease." So the Buddha sets the bar pretty high.

Robert: This has been really wonderful. Thank you very much, Ajahn.

Roshi Joan Halifax

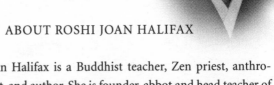

ABOUT ROSHI JOAN HALIFAX

Roshi Joan Halifax is a Buddhist teacher, Zen priest, anthropologist, and author. She is founder, abbot and head teacher of Upaya Zen Center, a Buddhist monastery in Santa Fe, New Mexico.

She studied for a decade with Zen teacher Seung Sahn, and was a teacher in the Kwan Um Zen School. She received the Lamp Transmission from Thich Nhat Hanh, and was given Inka by Roshi Bernie Glassman. A founding teacher of the Zen Peacemaker Order, her work and practice for more than three decades has focused on engaged Buddhism.

I first met Roshi Joan Halifax in 1987, when she brought Native American elder Leon Shenandoah to a gathering in Crestone, Colorado. It takes great skill to tend to the needs of such elders and then just (not Roshi) Joan demonstrated both an attentiveness and protectiveness for this great elder in her charge.

I had not spoken with her for 20 years. In that time she has done more work for the incarcerated and for environmental protection, becoming recognized as a master in the tradition of Zen. She is one of a few noted female Buddhist teachers today and I felt that her voice was an important one to hear in this work.

Our interview was held over Skype in the spring of 2006. I was at home and Roshi Joan had just come out of a retreat at her center in New Mexico.

THE INTERVIEW

Robert: I would first like to ask you about the Buddhist notion of this being a dark age. In your view, what is a dark age and what are the signs and conditions that would indicate that we are in one?

Roshi Joan: Well, I think mythologically speaking and psychologically speaking, the human psyche wants to to see things in terms of cycles, and this notion of a dark age points to something that, I think, is rather interesting. Instead of things happening in a cycle which is a seasonal vision, a dark age has to do with a model of steady decline from which there is no sense of rebirth.

So we have two models, models "A" and "B." There is the cyclical model with spring, summer, winter, fall, with rebirth in the spring, which is one way to describe our psychological condition and conditions on this planet and in our society. And there is this model of things getting steadily worse. So, you know, I think both models are interesting. Both models have their validity. I think that it is also interesting to look at the possibility that at some level we are always in a "dark age." There is always suffering and from another perspective this suffering is relative, from the point of the absolute, not inherent.

So, what is a dark age? It's an age of great suffering. Are we in a dark age? Yes, we are in a dark age. Is our experience different from 1,000 or 2,000 years ago? I rather think not.

If you look at the life of the Buddha, for example, there were tremendous social and cultural challenges during the era in which the Buddha lived. In fact, various configurations of that time were not so different to what we are experiencing now. It's just a matter of scale. The scale of suffering is much greater because of both the positive and negative perspective of our extreme connectivity.

Robert: Looking at some of these extreme aspects of it, probably if you believe in things like Atlantis and Lemuria, there have been civilizations that have come and gone…

Roshi Joan: I don't think you have to go back to Atlantis or that far. We do know, however, about Rome. The Inca, Mayan, early Chinese cultures – I mean, this is just the cycle of life – civilizations crash and burn and something comes up from their ashes.

Robert: I am sure that even in those times, as I think is the case now, there are people who witness and understand what is happening around them in their civilization, and there are others who are either not aware and think everything is OK or do not want to pay attention. It would seem that the number is few who strive and make efforts to remain conscious that such demises are occurring.

That said, the Chinese speak of the curse of living "in interesting times." What attitudes do you think need to be most dominant in people's minds for them to survive such times in positive ways?

Roshi Joan: Well, I think it is important to realize the truth of impermanence. This is a very powerful realization which allows you to embrace the fact that, yes, there may be suffering today, but who knows what will happen tomorrow?

Robert: Roshi, you are probably familiar with the Buddhist meal chant that ends with "may sickness, poverty, and warfare subside wherever we may be." Of these three problems, which do you think is possibly most pronounced today or, for that matter, in general throughout time, and how does it impact the other two?

Roshi Joan: I think that poverty is not a root cause by any means but is one of the reasons for warfare as well as sickness. But I think that these three, sickness, poverty, and warfare, are fairly external factors. I think we need to look more deeply into the human mind and the human heart to see the cause of these kinds of suffering.

Robert: So would you say that all three of these are important, but they are also just an expression of samsara (i.e. conditioned existence)?

Roshi Joan: Yes, but we are talking about something that has to do with a profound misperception or misunderstanding about the nature of reality.

Robert: So, you look at the things that are happening at this time; obviously it is natural for people to want to lessen that suffering. And, yes, from the Buddhist point of view, the most profound way to end this suffering is to offer the dharma – to cut through the root of this suffering. But, then again, you think of the quote of Mahatma Gandhi who said that "To a starving person, God comes in the form of bread." Some people want to do something to address sickness, others are more concerned with poverty or warfare – of these three, where do you think the greatest efforts should be made?

Roshi Joan: I think the first step is to stop. Don't do anything. Go within and stabilize the mind, and develop the quality of perception that allows you to actually understand what is happening within you and around us. I think that often we act from a place that is reactive; that is, not skillfully responsive. And I think that there are many beings that you can help along the way.

I think that the most important work is to help oneself and others to develop a mind, and heart, that is deeply stable and able to perceive that we are not separate from one another. So, if someone else is sick, we are sick. If someone else is impoverished, we are impoverished and we are joined to share our wealth. There is no way we could carry on warfare if we saw the truth that we are not separate from one another.

It's just this very deep sense of the hardened and separate self that gives rise to fundamental expressions of suffering.

Robert: It is always true that there is always the deeper aspect whenever we address these questions. We are directed back to the mind and try to understand the world around us through understanding the nature of the mind.

Roshi Joan: Yes…

Robert: And then we step out of our front door and try not to dissociate from what it is that we see.

Roshi Joan: Yes…

Robert: In which case, based on what you see, you do what you can. So there is no specific action that you can pinpoint as much as who you are, what you are, what you have available, and what you can do in the time that you are here. End of story.

Roshi Joan: Well I think that people have different scales of effectiveness. One expression, for sure, is that we take care of what we see before us.

Like Schumacher who coined the phrase, "Think globally, act locally." So, we have to take care of that which is in direct contact with us. But we can also think more globally. That is, we can do our very best to help transform social, political, and cultural policies that are oppressive and that are unjust.

Being more specific…You bring questions about sickness and drug addiction and abuse, and you ask what factors contribute to this problem. Of course, one of the factors is poverty. But poverty is not just material poverty. Drug addiction arises from a sense of psychological and spiritual poverty as well. So it's not just a matter of giving people money. It is also a matter of creating a deeper context of nourishment and enrichment that is not based on material things.

About pandemics – we have a pandemic of war, not just SARS or avian flu. Our own human greed is a kind of pandemic that is destroying the environment and is actually liberating these viruses from the safe quarters of the wilderness in which they have been found.

Again, there is a feeling that there are not suVicient resources to take care of an ever burgeoning population. But this is not just a matter of material resources. There is also a need of spiritual resources that can cultivate a basic satisfaction for what we have. The more we cut down and destroy our environment the more we unleash these lethal life forms which will be unleashed upon those who are destroying their environment.

Regarding malnutrition, the compliment to that is obesity which, again, comes from a sense of there not being enough.

I am here with my good friend, Brother David Steindl-Rast, who carries, in his pocket, napkins filled with leftover food that he could not eat at lunch, but he will consume as a snack later on. He is not just going to throw it away. This is a small example of sustainability. And so this vision of sustainability affects a vision of all these three questions of drug addiction, pandemics, and malnutrition. How do we live in balance and harmony with each other?

Of course, I think that the issue of population is a very important in this.

Robert: I guess the issues that come to me when looking at population have to do with religious perception of things like abortion, stem cell research, and birth control. What would you say is the Buddhist perception of these matters?

Roshi Joan: I think that from the Buddhist perspective, the concern is not just with the sanctity of human life, but the sanctity of all of life. If we take into account the sanctity of all of life, then we will understand that the expanding human population cannot be sustained by the life forms on this planet if we continue to pursue the current patterns of consumption. Issues related to abortion or choice, issues related to stem cell research, to euthanasia – whether to end life, hasten death, create life, yes, Teilhard de Chardin made it clear that with the increase of faculties of human consciousness there is an increase in responsibility. And I think that it is fundamental that human beings understand, with the kind of authority that we have in relation to these very fundamental questions about life, that we must also engage in a very deep and committed level of responsibility.

In fact, in looking at the questions you bring about environmental factors, when you say, "What do you see as the role of individual responsibility in addressing environmental and ecological concerns?" I would say that it is paramount.

Robert: Sure. The simplistic way of looking at these things would say that if we actually involve ourselves with birth control or stem cell research, we are somehow playing God. This is in contrast to the perspective that we have been endowed with the capacity to use this research intelligently. It has nothing to do with us usurping God's place as the first cause of all life but rather whether we can make life easier or more problematic for those around us.

Roshi Joan: Yes.

Robert: Much of the background behind the debate on these issues comes from a dualistic view that is expressed in the rise of fundamentalism, both in the East and the West. What do you see as the reasons for the growth of these faiths at this time?

Roshi Joan: I think that human beings typically like to polarize or identify with one side or another. And polarization is an expression of seeing the world in a very dualistic manner. It is very difficult to hold a position in the middle, and fundamentalism is, of course, an approach that is very interesting in that it basically posits a self and other. It is a very human position to take, but I don't think that it is a position that is going to lead to long-term harmonious survival.

Robert: How much of an impact do you think fundamentalism is having on the many political and social issues that are facing this planet right now?

Roshi Joan: I think it has a tremendous influence. I think that our own government is headed by people that are fundamentalist. I think that the major issues in the Middle East are the crux of the fundamentalist dilemma. It's us against them from the perspective of both sides of the fence. And, you know, this is this is a primitive form of perceiving and dealing with the world because it is fundamentally not based on a vision of harmony or inclusivity. It is based on a very reified sense that there is a self.

Robert: With respect to communities, I would say that, for example where we live, on the Central Coast of California, there is a growing evidence of fundamentalist influence on social and public policy.

Roshi Joan: Yes, this may be the case now, but again, things go in cycles. I would think that towards the end, Rome was probably pretty fundamentalist when it fell. So, I think that our own fundamentalist approach is leading us into tremendous problems: environmental, including pollution; social, creating a tremendous amount of psychological oppression for most individuals; problems in economies and whole populations, including the migrations, exiles, and refugees of warfare. All the problems we are seeing today are really coming out of what we could call adventitious suffering or stupidity – human beings not realizing that if we don't get along with all beings then the world will turn against us. You know we are just fouling our own nest, because we haven't perceived that we are a part of it.

Robert: Coming back to a more local perspective on all of this, Roshi… Because of this attitude, parents look at their children's education and the pressures to put the theological theory of intelligent design into the science curriculum, for example. In the case of my own son's school, there is overt proselytizing from fundamentalist students which creates a tremendous amount of peer pressure. What would you say to parents who don't necessarily want to mollycoddle their children, but want to genuinely protect them from pressure in these matters?

Roshi Joan: I think the most important thing a parent can do is to give their children a lot of love. You can't put your child in a bell glass to protect them from influences in the world. But I think you can model inclusivity and harmony. Your behavior with your child is of course through the expression of loving kindness and compassion. I don't think this is so much a cognitive and educational issue, but rather an affective issue. I think the basic message is to love your kids and model what it is to be love in the world.

Robert: I would like to move on to another issue and that is terrorism. How would you define terrorism?

Roshi Joan: I don't really think about terrorism very much. I know it is a great political buzzword and it is producing all kinds of bizarre behaviours. I can't really say much other than that it is the most pathological expression of fundamentalism.

Robert: OK, I can just leave that one right there. That is good enough. At the same time, I would like to address one aspect of this issue, because hopefully, some of the people who read this book may be living in places where they are surrounded by overt and heinous levels of aggression. Of course, you could say that happens in our own inner cities…

Roshi Joan: And it happens in our own prisons…

Robert: You are of course right. But can we address this question from the perspective of people dealing with bombs going off? What kind of attitude would you encourage people to have in order to inoculate themselves or give them some sense of stability? For some of these people cannot move for whatever reason from these situations.

Roshi Joan: I think that this is a very complex question. First, one needs to reconcile to the truth of one's own mortality, whether it is from old age or violence. I think one also has to accept the truth of suffering and that one lives in that situation. But, on the most practical level, one needs to deal with the stress in a very practical way; to do the best they can to take care of themselves and others in such dreadful conditions.

I can't imagine living like that. I mean, I have worked in the prison system and it is like being in a hell zone. I have even worked in maximum security. So I have some sense of what it is to be with people who lives are constantly threatened. One needs to have some kind of self-care in the midst of horrendous conditions and of course, if you do not have a practice that stabilizes the mind, if you don't have a view of impermanence, it becomes more difficult. You become much more subject to fear.

Robert: Were you teaching meditation in prison?

Roshi Joan: Yes I was.

Robert: So, from your own personal experience, were the people who were beginning to understand the value of meditation practice able to cope better than the others?

Roshi Joan: Yes, that seemed to be the case, as it also was when I worked with people with catastrophic illnesses. In such cases, having a very mature practice is helpful. It's rather difficult to get a diagnosis that you have got three months to live and then try to stabilize yourself in an already chaotic situation.

I think that what the stress does in these war zones, for many people, is that it aggravates the symptoms of fragility that is inherent to most people's lives. And, for some people, they are actually able to become more resilient in conditions that are horrible.

Robert: In the situations that you describe, you obviously saw both men and women who seemed to be doing OK. Other than teaching them meditation, did you observe something in their perspective or attitude that inoculated them more effectively?

Roshi Joan: I think positive attitudes and a positive adaptation to their very difficult circumstances give rise to an individual who has tremendous depth and strength. The opposite is the case for many individuals where their morale, as a result of the stress, diminishes their health and their will to live is decreased – the result is profound suffering. I think that both cases are true.

Robert: Looking at the next 100 years, seeing what you see around you, considering the kind of world that people find themselves in now, which of the issues we have discussed do you see being resolved, and which do you think will persist – other than the suffering of the mind?

Roshi Joan: Actually, Robert, I can't really answer this. These three – sickness, poverty, and warfare – are profoundly interconnected. War and sickness, and war and poverty, are like partners, so maybe we can look at them as three sides of a triangle. I think that with the increase of human sensitivity and human responsibility, the possibility of the diminution of these three forms of suffering is there. But I can't say when; we don't know whether there is going to be a catastrophic bifurcation where the environmental system collapses, a pandemic and the world population dies of some avian flu virus – I can't make those kind of prognostications. Of course, Jay Forrester did. The thing that we do know, from the point of view of complexity theories, is that a living system is robust because it has faced profound challenges, broken down, and learned how to repair itself. So, we are doing this at a more rapid rate than probably was the case with the global civilization of the past. So we might avoid the escape scenario from the planet earth where you take your problems with you, so to speak, as you seek an alternative universe because you ruined your own earth. What we are experiencing may just be a precursor to a level of robustness of planetary harmony and cooperation that is going to be extraordinary. And if that doesn't happen in the next few years… well, I don't think I am that silly…

Robert: Several years ago I met a reincarnated Canadian teacher by the name of Namgyal Rinpoche. He talked about the Aquarian Age going one of two ways. It can be where there is love and light, and a robust civilization emerges that is more awake. Or it can be a time of massive institutionalization and bureaucratization, but there would be what he called "pockets of light," these places where people would come together and the opportunity for transformation would be great, but in small communities, like sangha, and it wouldn't necessarily have an effect in changing society immediately.

Roshi Joan: Well, I think that is one model, but he probably offered that model in a time when the world wasn't so connected. But anyway, I think that it's a very nice view.

Robert: For many people, they are very discouraged, suicidal, even wanting to detach from what they see around them. Obviously that is an aspect of the dark age within their own minds, but at the same time people are reaching out and trying to find others of like mind. What words of encouragement would you offer these people?

Roshi Joan: I would tell them to take care of other people. Do something that is of benefit to others. I think that working with those who are less fortunate than oneself can be extremely healing of one's own self-centeredness, self-pity, and self-cherishing. I would also tell them to spend some time in the wilderness and to also spend some time doing a practice that engenders loving kindness so that they can begin to feel for others, but for themselves as well. And to see this life as fleeting in all cases. We have so little time on this earth. The most meaningful thing that we can do is to find a way to benefit others, even in the most immediate or small way. That's probably what I would say. It's simple.

Robert: Thank you, Roshi.

Ven. Thubten Chodron

ABOUT VEN. THUBTEN CHODRON

Born in 1950, Thubten Chodron grew up near Los Angeles. She graduated with a B.A. in history from the University of California at Los Angeles in 1971. After traveling through Europe, North Africa and Asia for one and a half years, she received a teaching credential and went to the University of Southern California to do postgraduate work in education while working as a teacher in the Los Angeles city school system.

In 1975, she attended a meditation course given by Ven. Lama Yeshe and Ven. Zopa Rinpoche, and subsequently went to their monastery in Nepal to continue to study and practice Buddha's teachings. In 1977, she received the *sramanerika* (novice) ordination, and in 1986, went to Taiwan to take the *bhikshuni* (full) ordination.

She studied and practiced Buddhism of the Tibetan tradition for many years in India and Nepal, and directed the spiritual program at Lama Tzong Khapa Institute in Italy for about two years. She studied for three years at Dorje Pamo Monastery in France and was resident teacher at Amitabha Buddhist Center in Singapore. Ven. Chodron was a co-organizer of the "Life as a Western Buddhist Nun" event and took part in the conferences of Western Buddhist teachers with H.H. Dalai Lama in 1993 and 1994. She was present during the Jewish delegation's visit to Dharamsala, India, in 1990, which was the basis for the book and documentary, *The Jew in the Lotus*, and she is keen on inter-religious dialogue. She has also attended several of the "Mind-Life" conferences in which scientists and H.H. Dalai Lama discuss similarities and differences between science and Buddhism.

Ven. Chodron lived and taught in Seattle with Dharma Friendship Foundation (DFF) for nine years. Currently, she is founding Sravasti Abbey, a monastery in the USA. She travels worldwide to give talks about Buddhism and to teach meditation.

When I was doing my interview with Tenzin Robert Thurman and mentioned my desire to have more female voices included for the book, he mentioned Ven. Thubten Chodron. Because of worklife, I must confess that I have had less time to read than I would like – and therefore had never read any of Venerable's works.

Because she was leading a retreat on compassion when he mentioned her, it took a few weeks for me to make contact with her at her center, Sravasti Abbey. What is missing from the interview, recorded through Skype in early 2007, is the personal banter that went back and forth between us about where we had been, who we knew, and how similar our backgrounds were and showing almost no degrees of separation. It felt like I was interviewing a long-time friend. It is, therefore, both an honor and pleasure to include her here.

THE INTERVIEW

Robert: Thank you, Ven. Chodron, for being willing to participate in this book project.

From the questionnaire that I sent you, you can see that parts of it have to do with seeking understanding from the various teachers on a Buddhist philosophical and cosmological view of the times we live in. For example, I have received answers from many of the teachers about their perspective on what, in Buddhism, is called a dark age and whether or not they think we are in one, and what that means, practically speaking. Then there is my desire to get more ordinary, personal perspectives on the kinds of issues that the average person would hear about if they turn on FOX News or CNN: fundamentalism, terrorism, global warming, and various other issues and their buzzwords that create tension and strife in our culture and society. I would like you to feel comfortable in sharing your perspectives on such philosophical and practical issues based on your training and life experience, knowing that the intention of this book is to reach a general – rather than Buddhist – audience.

To begin, what are your thoughts about the notion of a dark age?

Ven. Chodron: I have heard this time being described as a "degenerate age" rather than dark age. I try to be sensitive to terminology and not use the word "dark" to mean "negative."

The thought-training teachings describe our time as a "degenerate age," in the sense that sentient beings' disturbing emotions and wrong views are strong. The Kalachakra teachings prophesize a devastating war, but the good forces from the kingdom of Shambhala are to win the day.

To tell you the truth, I don't find this way of thinking helpful. I do not let my mind adopt the way of thinking that says, "This is a degenerate age. Things are getting worse and everything is falling apart. There is so much wrong with the world – so much war and horror. What a terrible state we are in!" I don't find that frame of mind helpful. The media plays on the fear and dread that come from adopting that view, the "It's the end of the world" Armageddon way of thinking. I don't buy into it. So, from my perspective, is it a "degenerate time"? To be frank, all of samsara [cyclic existence] is degenerate. Samsara, by definition, is basically flawed. If we expect perfection, then anything will appear degenerate in contrast. However, if we give up the unrealistic expectations that somehow sentient beings, plagued by ignorance, hostility, and attachment, will live in a perfect world, we'll see goodness around us and will be able to increase that goodness. In addition, we'll aim for real happiness, which is not to be found in samsara. Actual joy is born from transforming our minds, from spiritual practice that increases wisdom and compassion.

The situation we're in is what we are in. It exists due to the karma we created in the past. It is also an opportunity for us to act for the benefit of others; to contribute to the well-being of others in the world and create good karma that will influence our future experiences. Accepting the situation for what it is, and seeing it as the environment in which we will develop equal love and compassion for all sentient beings, brings more happiness now. It also enables us to create the causes for future happiness.

The reason why I really recoil from this terminology of "dark" or "degenerate" age is that it becomes a self-fulfilling prophecy. This way of thinking makes us suspicious and afraid, which creates more ill will in society. The media plays on our fear and the American public buys into it. I refuse to accept that world-view. It is neither accurate nor beneficial.

Robert: Seeing what people are exposed to by the media as hype and that people are buying into it, beyond the methods of contemplation and meditation encouraged by Buddhist tradition, how else would you inoculate people to become more resistant to an indoctrination which is freaking them out?

Ven. Chodron: The first thing I would tell them is to turn off the television set and the radio and to get in touch with the goodness and willingness to help that they have inside. People need to be much more careful and mindful of how they relate to the media and how they allow media to influence their lives and the lives of their children. The media persuades us of a world-view that is false. What is that world-view? Having more possessions will make you happy. Having more sex will make you happy. Telling off the people who harm you will make you happy. The more money you have, the more successful you are. Terrorists, rapists, and kidnappers are around the corner, trying to harm you, so don't trust anyone. Bombing your enemies will bring peace. Is this true? All we need to do is look at our own experience and we'll see that it is not true.

People are exposed to hundreds, if not thousands, of advertisements daily. The underlying theme of these advertisements is, "You are deficient as you are. You need something that you don't have. You need to be different than you are." They give us the message that happiness is outside of ourselves. It has nothing to do with who we are on the inside. All of those messages tell us that to be happy, you have to be young and have a lot of sex, because sex is the ultimate happiness. To be attractive sexually, you have to wear certain clothes, drive a particular type of car, look a certain way, and so on. Is any of this true? We idolize youth, but no one is getting younger; we're all aging. Are people really happier having more sex? Or does this world-view make people more fearful of being inadequate or unattractive?

This consumerist world-view feeds attachment and dissatisfaction. When we don't get what we want (because we are supposed to want all of those things outside ourselves – consumer products, sex, people, love, whatever), then we get angry. From anger come many of the other problems we see in society.

Those of us who don't want to have this world-view will pay attention to how the media conditions us, and we will thoughtfully, and with discernment, consciously choose how we let the media influence us. We deliberately remind ourselves daily of what we believe and how we want to train our mind. The disadvantages of adopting the world-view, believing that objects of attachment will make us happy, is that if we don't get what we want, we think we have every right to take it from somebody else or to destroy whoever impedes us from getting what we want. This is what is enacted on television programs. They're all about attachment and violence. When we watch them, they condition us with their world-view and as a result, our greed and anger increase. Such clinging attachment and anger motivate us to act in harmful ways. Not seeing that our own harmful emotions create discord, inequality, and injustice, we label this a "degenerate age" and think that others are the source of the problem. Thinking the world is in an awful state makes us despair and fall into depression. We medicate these feelings by being greedy and buying more things or by having an extramarital affair. Or we think that expressing them will alleviate the bad feelings, so we get angry and shout at our family. Or we drink and drug and do all of the above. And thus the cycle continues.

If we don't have that world-view, or don't want to be conditioned by that world-view, we avoid reading the magazines and newspapers or watching the TV programs that propagate dissatisfaction, fear, and violence. When we meet people who have been conditioned by that world-view, we are aware that they mean well but we don't follow their advice. For example, let's say you prefer to spend time talking to your children instead of climbing the corporate ladder, and other people say to you, "What do you mean you prefer to work at a lower-paying job so that you'll have more free time? You should work hard now and then retire early and enjoy." With wisdom, you see that it's not that simple, that if you work hard now you'll wind up with more commitments and obligations. In the meantime, your children will grow up and you'll miss out on really getting to know them. You'll miss out on helping them to grow up to be kind human beings who feel loved and who know how to give love to others. So keeping your priorities clear in your mind, you do what is important and don't mind what others say about your life.

I advocate that we live according to our values. To know what our values are, we need time to reflect, and to have that time, we need to disengage from the TV, radio, Internet. Nowadays that can be hard. People have so much sense stimulation from the time they are children that they have forgotten how to be peaceful and quiet. In fact, they feel strange if there is not an abundance of noise and activity around.

We don't watch TV at the Abbey where I live. Because I travel a lot to teach, once in a while I'll watch part of a movie on the transoceanic flights. The scenes change so much faster than when I was a kid, and I can't keep up. Because kids are used to watching the scenes in movies change so quickly, it's no wonder that there is so much ADD or ADHD.

Robert: Or that they expect things to happen immediately.

Ven. Chodron: Yes. Everything happens so quickly. So you become conditioned like that from the time you are very little and you are hooked on a diet of sensory overstimulation. As a result, you are out of touch with who you are. You have not taken the time to ask yourself what you really believe because the consumer society is constantly conditioning you and giving you an identity. This is especially true in the West, but it is happening more and more in the developing world as well. There is never any time to stop and think, "Do I believe what they are telling me?" and "What do I think is important in my life?" and "What do I want to be the meaning of my life?"

In brief, there are two factors. The first is that we are conditioned by society and its values, and secondly, we buy into the conditioning and do not think for ourselves about what is important. Then, in fact, we become part of the society that conditions children and adults to be overly busy. The situation cycles on from there.

Instead, we should think about what we believe and live according to it as much as we can. We don't propagate our world-view by standing on street corners, but if we walk our talk, people who are open will notice it and connect with us. That happens to me a lot when I travel. I'm just being me, but people see the monastic robes and I guess they watch how I act and they'll come up and ask questions or talk to me about their lives.

Robert: What you are saying is quite practical. You are not talking about any intensive meditative practice per se, but rather the simple willingness to be more active in your own life regarding the influences you have in your life. You're asking us to think about whether we want those influences or not, and then to take some time to actually reflect on what really matters to us personally. For example, when we watch TV, we can examine how what we are watching makes us feel and whether or not it agrees with or supports what we believe about life.

Ven. Chodron: Yes.

Robert: I noted your comment about not going onto the street corner with your beliefs. This segues into a question I have about fundamentalism, because I observe that if people are not being inundated with a consumer, material-based world-view, *and* if they do not have some tradition or education to develop their abilities to be more contemplative, there is the tendency in our society to seek more simplistic answers. Thus, there appears to be a growing interest in fundamentalist views in the world. What are your thoughts on this and how you think fundamentalism is influencing our current situation?

Ven. Chodron: Fundamentalism is a reaction to modernity. Things have changed so quickly due to technology. The structure of the family has been challenged and has disintegrated due to the pressures of the global economy. The comfort of small communities and community life has changed due to transportation and telecommunications that enable us to go to places we couldn't visit before, and to communicate with people who we don't live with all over the world. So how people think of themselves has changed. Most people don't really have a sense of who they want to be. They are fed a stream of television propaganda about what they are supposed to be. But nobody is that. Everybody looks at the characters on TV shows or in movies and thinks, "I should be like them, but I am not like them. They are young and attractive and interesting; I'm aging and not such an interesting person." People think that they should be other than who they are, but they can't be that gorgeous beauty or that spectacular athlete that they see on TV or in magazines. So they look for something that will give them an identity, someone who will tell them what to be and what to do in order to feel worthwhile.

If you join a group that has a strong identity, then as an individual you will have an identity. In addition, you will have a group to belong to; you won't be alone in this confusing world with all of its choices. You will be protected from the "bad" people who lurk behind every corner. Furthermore, you will have a purpose that seems to be more meaningful than just consuming more and more.

A lot of religious fundamentalism is a reaction to being overly stimulated by the message that "craving and desire bring happiness" – this message brings on dissatisfaction and thus depression. In addition, fundamentalism provides a very quick solution to your scattered social life and a simplistic analysis of what is wrong and how to remedy it. When you feel dislocated, simplistic doctrine taught by a powerful leader gives you a feeling of belonging, a feeling of meaning, and some direction in life. Because you have been conditioned by the media to not think so much, then the leaders of fundamentalist movements can tell you things and you don't do much analysis. You follow because it's easy, because they are a symbol of power when you feel confused. In any case, you are not used to thinking deeply about things. Only now instead of the media feeding you a version of reality, the fundamentalist movement is.

While it superficially seems that there are so many fundamentalist movements, actually they are all very similar. If there were a convention of fundamentalists from all over the world, I think they would get along very well because they think alike. They just have different beliefs and names that they latch onto, different causes that they are attached to, but their way of thinking is remarkably alike.

Robert: So in that regard, you don't see much of a difference between the various fundamentalist movements worldwide?

Ven. Chodron: Not too much. They hold different beliefs and have somewhat different conditioning due to the different scriptures, cultures, and circumstances. But in the sense of offering a simple analysis in which the problems we face are due to other people and the solution is to follow the instructions of an external authority – be it God, Allah, or a political or religious leader – they are very similar. People are looking for meaning and direction in life and would like to have a quick and relatively easy solution to problems. From this viewpoint, we can see there are also fundamentalist Democrats, fundamentalist Buddhists, and even fundamentalist vegetarians! It all boils down to the belief that problems are due to other people and their ignorance, and the solution is to convince others of the correctness of one's own views. Why should others hold one's own views? Because they are the correct ones.

Fundamentalists of all types believe they are being compassionate in their words and actions. They don't see what they are thinking and doing as intolerant, but truly believe that it is their duty to convert everyone to their way of thinking. They think, "My way of thinking is the right way. I have compassion and care for you, therefore I am going to try and get you to think the way I think." Violent fundamentalists believe that they are being compassionate in freeing the world from what they consider to be harmful people who have dangerous beliefs (i.e. beliefs that are different from one's own). But the way fundamentalists go about their conversion attempts is permeated with disrespect for others' cultures, beliefs, customs, habits, and in some cases others' physical safety.

One thing that attracted me to Buddhism was my teachers saying that a diversity of religions is good. Why? Because people have different dispositions and interests. One religion is not capable of meeting the needs of everyone, whereas if there is a diversity, then people can choose the religious beliefs that make the most sense to them. Since all religions teach ethical conduct and kindness to others, people will practice these if they understand the meaning of their own religion correctly. Of course, if people don't understand the purpose of their own religion, or actively misunderstand it, it's another case altogether.

In the light of honoring diversity, I must say that my words in this interview are my personal opinions. Please do not confuse my personal opinions on political and social matters with Buddhist doctrine. Buddhists are free to vote for whom they wish; we do not have a social and political dogma that everyone must adhere to in order to be Buddhists. I'm simply applying what I know of Buddhist principles and values to the questions you pose. Other Buddhists may have other ideas. These are all our personal opinions.

Robert: And to some extent they think, "I am doing you a favor if I annihilate you because, as an infidel, you would never go to heaven anyway." Looking at the current wars and debacle in the Middle East, some have likened it to being a modern Crusade, a battle between fundamentalist Christianity and Islam. Some have made it more specific in saying that it is war between the fundamentalist American administration and Islam. Others look at this as just a cover for what they think is really going on, that being modern corporate greed. From your perspective, what do you see as the primary factors in this conflict? How much do you think it just boils down to war profiteering and corporate greed or a real battle of fundamentalist ideologies? Or is it a combination of the two?

Ven. Chodron: In college I majored in history where we were asked to consider these various factors. As a young person I was shocked to discover that in European history, during almost every generation, people killed each other in the name of God. There were so many religious wars and, in some cases, they were masks for leaders' greed for wealth and power. I think the roots of such problems go much deeper than just religious philosophy and much deeper than just corporate greed. It seems to me that it has to do with people's need to feel worthwhile and respected. Our self-grasping ignorance wants recognition that we exist and that we are worthwhile. According to society's values, one way to gain respect and a feeling of self-worth is to have possessions. I am not saying that that is correct, but that's the way people think.

Several centuries ago, the Islamic world was much more advanced than the Western world, more cultured and economically well-to-do. Minorities and women generally had more freedom in Islamic countries than in Christian ones. But the Industrial Revolution in the West changed the relationship between Islamic and Christian counties. Europe surged ahead materially and Islamic countries had a hard time catching up. This brought on feelings of inferiority because they lacked the same technology, industrial products, and consumer goods. Meanwhile the West dove into materialism and consumerism, which we see has harmed family structure, increased substance abuse and sexual freedom (or promiscuity, depending on how you see it). Muslims look at this and think, "We are not respected because we haven't caught up materially, but we don't want the cultural disintegration that materialism and consumerism have brought about in the West." There is no other model for how to modernize – how to take the best from technology and the best of traditional values. This sets the stage for Islamic fundamentalism. I believe people in the USA who have turned to fundamental Christianity feel the same displacement in the modern world. Technology is bringing a great deal of change very quickly, and as societies we have not thought of where we are going with this. People are looking for something secure and predictable. They are also searching for some ethical standards and common customs that bring them together.

Robert: Would you say this is also an underlying matter of just plain human pride?

Ven. Chodron: Yes, that is involved as well. So often, people would much rather die to protect their honor than risk their life to guard their possessions. Honor is your worth, your value as a human being; it is more valuable than possessions.

I'm not justifying fundamentalism, but if we can understand how the people who turn to it think, we will be able to communicate with them better. See it from their side: they don't have what the Western world has materially and their traditional ways of life – the emphasis on family, the traditional power structure in society – is being challenged by the West. How can Islamic societies see themselves as worthwhile and worthy of respect in their own and others' eyes? This may be part of the issue from the Islamic side.

From the side of the West – particularly in my country, the USA – there is a lot of greed and arrogance. We arrogantly flaunt our material and technological success, and unfortunately we export the worst part of our culture, not the best. I've traveled in and lived in Third World countries. What do they see when they finally get TV in their village? American movies with sex, violence, and extraordinary opulence. Kung fu movies. What about exporting our compassion, our respect for cultural diversity? What about enacting our values of justice and equality in our foreign policy?

I don't think the conflict in the Middle East has to do with our wanting Iraqis, Palestinians, and others to have democracy and freedom. After all, the current administration is curtailing democracy, freedom, and justice in our own country! It seems to me that the conflict in the Middle East and Iraq is over oil and although I am loath to say this...

Robert: I guarantee you, Venerable, that if you are about to make a politically incorrect statement, considering some of the other comments from Rinpoches and teachers, you are in good company. [Laughter.]

Ven. Chodron: OK, from my personal observation on a human level, I think that George W Bush had a personal grudge against Saddam Hussein, arising because his father did not unseat Hussein. Of course, Bush was not consciously aware of it: most people think they have good motivations. Bush believes that what he is doing is right.

In addition, the American public is attached to its comfortable lifestyle that depends on oil. We are unwilling to cut back on our oil use and consumer goods – in short, on our disproportional consumption of the world's resources – in order to share with other people in the world. That has fueled the war as well.

Robert: Looking at the notion of terrorism and the way it is being used in the media, how would you define this word and what a terrorist act is?

Ven. Chodron: Terrorism is in the eye of the beholder. I was born Jewish, part of the first generation of Jews born after the Holocaust. As a result, supporting the underdog, helping those who were persecuted or oppressed, was very much a part of my upbringing.

In the late 1990s, some Israeli dharma practitioners in India invited me to go to Israel to teach the dharma and I happily accepted. Most Israeli Buddhists are liberal politically, like American convert Buddhists. On one of the visits to Israel, some of my friends took me to an old British prison in the north of Israel where the British had imprisoned many Jews who wanted Israel to become a nation and were working in various ways towards that goal. Some of them were Zionists who fought the British in order to be able to stay in Palestine. They were arrested, sentenced, and executed at this prison. This prison is now a museum commemorating the struggle for independence. In it was the place where these Jews were hanged, and on the walls were pictures of these men together with the stories of what they did and why the British arrested them and imprisoned them. Some of them had sabotaged British officials, attacked buses, and planned bombings. After reading some of their stories, I turned to my friends and commented, "These guys were terrorists, weren't they?" And my friends looked shocked and one of them said, "No, they were patriots."

That is why I said terrorism is in the eye of the beholder. What one person considers terrorism, another considers patriotism. For example, wasn't the Boston Tea Party terrorism? Weren't some of the Europeans' attacks on the Native Americans terrorism? Terrorism is labeled from the perspective of the people who receive harm that they felt was unfair, harsh, and harmed civilians. Seen from that perspective, terrorism is not anything new. What is new is that it is the first time that middle-class America is experiencing it.

Robert: One of the hopes for this book is that it will go to countries and be read by people who might be in situations with acts of terror happening around them; where they witness bombings and on a day-to-day basis may suffer personal fear of an act that might harm them or the people that they love. What would you encourage people in those situations to do? In many of the "hot spots" on the planet – Iraq, Darfur, and other places – it does not seem that such terror is going to go away soon. In what ways can we help people to cope with these situations?

Ven. Chodron: I have never experienced what people in Iraq are experiencing, so I don't know if I could give advice that would be helpful.

Robert: I appreciate your candor, Venerable. But at the same time, when you go to Israel, you have met people who live in Tel Aviv and have to make choices as to which bus they feel most safe on and which market they feel safest going to for groceries.

Ven. Chodron: In a way, I think it is a little presumptuous of me to give advice about a situation that I have not lived through. My suggestions would be merely theoretical, never having had to face those challenges myself.

Having said that, if I ask myself – and I have definitely thought about this – what would happen if I were in that situation? Circumstances can change very quickly and without notice, I could find myself in that situation. So I think about what I would say or do if I were to be faced with a terrorist activity of some sort or a fearful situation – how would I practice? From this perspective, I could share with others ideas I've had about how I could bring my dharma practice into that type of situation. Of course, when a frightful event happens, we're never sure that we will have the presence of mind to think of dharma methods, or if we will fall back on old habits of fear and panic. So I'm not going to pretend to be sure that I'd able to practice what I preach.

Robert: You're just walking us through your own process.

Ven. Chodron: Yes. I would try to focus on the kindness of sentient beings – which sounds like the total opposite of what is happening in that situation. But that is exactly the point. What is the opposite of hatred, fear, panic, and anger – the emotions that would automatically arise in the minds of most of us? Strong positive emotions are needed, and in this case, I would try to remember the kindness of sentient beings and generate feelings of warmth, affection, and compassion for them. From a Buddhist perspective, when we look back over beginning-less previous lives, we see that all sentient beings have been our parents, friends, and relatives, and have been kind to us. They brought up us and taught us all the skills we have. In addition, in this life, too, everyone has been kind; we are intricately interrelated in society and we depend on others for our food, clothing, shelter, and medicine – the four requisites for life. When we are aware of being the recipient of such tremendous kindness from others, automatically we feel kindly in return. In addition, when we think that all sentient beings are just like us in wanting to be happy and to be free from suffering, we can't push them away mentally or emotionally.

When we think they are bound by their ignorance, mental afflictions, and karma, compassion naturally arises. I would see that the people who are trying to hurt me are suffering at that very moment and that's why they are doing what they are doing. If they were happy, they wouldn't be doing what they are doing. Nobody harms anyone when they are happy. So these people are unhappy. I know what it's like to be miserable and this is what these people are experiencing, even though they may mask it by threatening others in order to feel powerful. So actually, compassion is a more appropriate response than fear and hatred to those who are suffering.

If I can feel that kind of equality with them – that we all want to be happy and free of suffering, that we are in this boat of samsara together – and if I can see them as having been kind to me in the past, then my mind will not make them into an enemy. And, if my mind does not make them into an enemy, I won't feel afraid. The feeling of fear is the biggest terror of terrorism. If you get hurt, that event doesn't last for a long time. But fear can last a long time and causes tremendous suffering. We fear what has not happened; we fear what does not yet exist. That fear is a product of our mind. Nevertheless, fear is excruciatingly painful. So in a dangerous situation, I would do my utmost to avoid letting my mind fall into a state of fear.

When we feel kind towards others, with love and compassion in our hearts, there is no space for fear or anger. Then there is peace in our hearts. Fear and hatred won't solve the problem of being in a stressful situation in which our life is in danger. In fact, they will make it worse: first, we aren't thinking clearly and could easily do something that exacerbates the situation. Second, even if I were to die, I would rather die with compassion and a free heart, not with anger.

Those are the methods I would use to deal with a threatening person or people: think of their kindness, remember that they are suffering, contemplate that we are equal in wanting happiness and not wanting suffering. More specifically, from my Buddhist training, I would remind myself of their Buddha potential: that these people possess the clear light mind, they have the empty nature of the mind. Under all the commotion of their lives and the chaos of the situation is buried the primordial clear light mind. If they could realize that, all this confusion wouldn't be going on. However, being completely overwhelmed by ignorance, anger, and attachment at this very moment, even though they want happiness they are creating the causes of unhappiness for themselves and for others. So there is nobody to hate here. How can we hate people who are overwhelmed by ignorance and mental afflictions and aren't even aware that they are harming themselves by harming others?

In addition, these living beings are just karmic appearances. If I could see them as such, there would be space in my mind; I would not be grasping so strongly to the view of inherent existence. I would see that they are not solid, "concrete" people. In fact, they are karmic bubbles. And I, too, am a karmic bubble, just an appearance created by causes and conditions. Furthermore, our karma brought us together: my karma definitely had a role in putting me in this situation and since the situation is unpleasant, certainly it was negative karma created by my self-centered attitude that is the culprit. So here we are, two karmic bubbles wandering in the confusion of samsara. There is nobody to hate here. There is nobody to be afraid of. It's a situation that calls for compassion above all else.

Robert: In some ways you are giving the reader a variation on the Four Immeasurables. [A classic Mahayana prayer that reads:

> May all beings have happiness and its causes.
> May all beings be free from suffering and its causes.
> May they never be separated from the great happiness
>   free of suffering.
> May they dwell in equanimity free from attachment,
>   aggression, and prejudice.]

You are also implying that if someone took time each day to practice mindfulness of those four, their mind would be clearer and more compassionate. In that case, when they left their house, they wouldn't be so afraid. If they faced a dangerous situation, they might just have more resourcefulness to act more constructively and wisely than the average person caught in their own panic. They might be able to prevent the situation from happening altogether, or at least they could make sure that the least number of people were harmed.

Ven. Chodron: Definitely. Because when our mind is under the influence of fear or anger, there's not much we can do in a situation. But if we can find commonality with those that threaten us, we are clearer, and if we can then point out some type of commonality to those who might harm us, we might be able to calm the situation. People find it much harder to harm others if they feel that they share things in common with them.

Robert: If speaking is one of the options in that situation…

Ven. Chodron: Yes, or whatever way you can find to point out a connection that you have with them.

Robert: Venerable, I would like to come around to another point if I may. Many Buddhist prayers express the wish for sickness, poverty, and warfare to end. In reflecting on these three challenges and causes of suffering for people, which do you think stands out most today? How do you see that one fueling the other two?

Ven. Chodron: I have to rewrite the question before answering it. From my perspective, ignorance, clinging attachment, and hostility are the sources of sickness, poverty, and war. That said, if we look at those three results, I think that poverty is the main one because when poverty is rampant, people do not feel respected and they do not have access to what they need to sustain their lives. When people lack resources, they cannot take care of their health and illness follows. When people are poor, oppression and prejudice are often involved and thus fighting erupts. In addition, if someone is poor and falls ill, they cannot receive proper treatment, and if the poor are trapped in a war zone they do not have the resources to flee to safety.

Poverty not only affects the poor. It also affects the rich because we live in an interdependent society. If we have enough but live in a society where people are poor, how do we feel about that? How do we feel about having possessions, education, and opportunities that other people don't have? How do we feel about social structures that favor our group over others? We could easily have been born in another group, and our present situation could change in any moment – so it's not the case that we or anyone else is guaranteed happiness in the future.

The rich have their own type of suffering. For example, I have taught in many countries, among them Guatemala and El Salvador. The middle-class and wealthy people there live behind barbed wire, just like the inmates at the prisons where I work. The well-to-do houses in those countries are surrounded by high walls and circles of barbed wire. Security guards stand at the gates, and the residents inside live in fear of being robbed or, in some cases, even kidnapped due to their wealth. These people are prisoners; they imprison themselves to protect themselves from the poor. To me, that constitutes suffering – the misery of the wealthy.

In the US, the very wealthy can't walk down the streets. You and I have so much freedom because we aren't wealthy. I can walk down the street and no one will try to kidnap me. If I had children – which I don't – they could go to a public school and play at the park. But the very wealthy and their families don't have that freedom. Their kids don't have freedom because they are rich. With wealth comes another kind of suffering.

Robert: There's probably not a government structure on the planet that doesn't favor some and disfranchise others, either by design or not. If you were to educate the wealthy and advantaged on the dilemma you are describing, what would you say to them? Or let's say you were asked to testify to Congress on the matter of war profiteering and how it is affecting people, what is the most insightful and beneficial way to approach these powers?

Ven. Chodron: Whenever a situation is already happening, it is difficult to get people to listen and it is hard to work with your own mind as well. For that reason, I advocate preventative measures, and that begins with the education of children.

Let's educate children on how to share and cooperate with others, how not to make differences of opinions into conflicts, and how to resolve conflicts that do inevitably arise when human beings are together. At present the educational system stresses the learning of facts and skills, and neglects teaching how to be a kind person and how to get along with people – in other words, how to be a good citizen of this planet. I was an elementary school teacher before becoming a nun, so this is something dear to my heart.

Kids need to learn human values, and these can be taught in a secular way, without preachers being in public schools (separation of church and state is very important!). If we want good citizens, we have to teach secular human values beginning in childhood. I would like to see the educational system emphasize this because when we train kids to be able to open their eyes and see the situation of others, when those kids grow into adults they will have more empathy. When people are more empathetic, they will not be so blind to others' needs and concerns. They will not be apathetic and will not exploit others. This relates to what I was saying before about all sentient beings being similar in wanting happiness and not wanting suffering: kids can understand that.

Once, somebody asked me to a luncheon with some wealthy people who weren't Buddhists: he thought they would be interested in meeting a Buddhist nun and asked me to give a short talk after lunch. I spoke about all beings being equal in wanting happiness and not wanting suffering. We all suffer from aging, sickness, and death, and we all love our families and don't want our families or ourselves to be hurt. We all want to be respected. By the end of the talk, the feeling in the room and the look on these people's faces had changed. Their hearts were opened just hearing a short talk. I wish these things could be said in front of the Congress or at an NRA convention; it resonates so deeply within us as human beings. So often all they hear from society and the media is the view that "Something outside of me is going to make me happy" and "It's an adversarial system and everything somebody else gets I don't have." On the news, they seldom hear of events where people help each other; TV programs seldom illustrate positive human interactions and human respect. Where do people see examples of patience and kindness? How can children learn these without seeing examples of them?

Media people say they report what people want to hear, but it seems to me that they hype up scandals and violence to sell their publications. So the public has become starved of hearing about goodness. That's why people who aren't Buddhist flock to see H.H. Dalai Lama. Because who else is going to just give them some message of basic human peace and goodness? Just hearing a short talk on how to see others with love and compassion relaxes their minds. They get in touch with something positive inside themselves and can see that others also have internal goodness. They become more optimistic. With this kind of view in their minds, their behavior changes.

Robert: You speak about the Buddhist notion of goodness, that we are basically good and that we actually know what is best, whether we are willing to admit to it or not, and that if you just focus on goodness, kindness, and human commonality, then people will give themselves permission to do what needs to be done rather than succumb because they were badgered to do so.

Ven. Chodron: Exactly, because Americans are very individualistic and do not like to be told what they should do. When they do something out of obligation or because they feel guilty, they feel pushed, whereas, when people get in touch with their own human values and human goodness, naturally they will express that and act according to it without others telling them what they should do.

This is very evident in the prison work I'm engaged in. The inmates teach me so much – much more than I teach them. Some of the men I write to have done the crimes that terrify me the most. Yet, when I get to know them, we are just two human beings and I am not afraid of them. While the "get tough on crime" movement portrays inmates as monsters, they are human beings like everyone else. They want to be happy and to be free of suffering, and most of them have seen a lot of suffering in their lives. They tell me about their lives, what it is like to be them. We discuss our values, emotions, and behavior from a dharma perspective.

Robert: Which would never come out if you told them what they should do.

Ven. Chodron: Exactly. The following isn't a general statement about all inmates. But the inmates who write to me are sensitive and thoughtful. When they look at the war in Iraq, their hearts go out to the civilians who are being adversely affected. Their hearts go out to our troops, who are often young men from lower-class families who think joining the military will be their ticket out of poverty. One inmate told me about seeing a little Iraqi girl on TV. She was horribly injured due to a bomb blast. Then a week later, on a TV special about a hospital in Iraq, he saw her in a hospital bed with a cast on. She looked so much better that he started crying for joy.

One inmate, who is in a dreadful prison in Illinois, was working in the prison kitchen. A little calico cat came around from time to time. She hadn't been around for a while and they were afraid that something had happened to her. One day she appeared again, and the inmates were so delighted to see her again – these big rough tough men who were in for murder – their hearts just melted when they saw that little cat. They took food from their own plates and went out to feed the cat. They were cooing and playing with her. This shows that we all have human kindness that comes out when we see another living being that we connect with.

Robert: Venerable, I would like to focus on a specific issue that you probably saw a good deal of in the prison population and that affects the population at large. That issue is drug addiction. What is your understanding of drug addiction in this country and what do you see as some of the antidotes that society can offer to deal with this problem that seems to be getting larger?

Ven. Chodron: I would like to broaden this to include alcohol addiction as well. Even though alcohol is legal, it does just as much damage.

Robert: Sure. That would be fine. We could go into the use and abuse of prescription medications as well.

Ven. Chodron: About 99 percent of the inmates I write to were under the influence of alcohol or drugs when they did the crime that landed them in prison. There's a battery of issues on an individual level, some of which we talk about. These are personal issues of the individual: people not feeling good about themselves, not feeling worthwhile, feeling pressured to be better than they are, different from how they are. Some of this is fed to us from the media, some is from the assumptions that ordinary people act on, some comes from the schools. In any case, the general message is that we are supposed to be a certain way and we aren't that. We are lacking and inadequate in one way or another. We need something – the items that are being advertised, a relationship, or whatever – to make us whole and good people. This breeds low self-esteem, and drugs and alcohol are quick ways to numb the discomfort that comes from the lack of self-confidence. Depression, feelings of unworthiness or of being bad – these feelings come about in a variety of ways and are often due to multiple causes. Family dynamics and interactions are certainly a factor: domestic violence, parental substance abuse, physical or sexual abuse of children, poverty – these are a few.

Another element is society's blindness to policies that can benefit us as a whole. It's sad; people want to lower the drug and alcohol rate, but they also advocate welfare cuts for poor families and single moms. They don't understand that increasing financial pressure on poor families who are already stressed will only increase the drug and alcohol rate. Parents will be absent from the family, so children lack a sense of belonging or of being loved.

In addition, voters don't want to spend more money on schools, education, and extracurricular activities for children and teenagers because they say this will increase their taxes. People who don't have children ask why their taxes should pay for the education of other people's children. This makes me sad because they don't see the inter-relationship among people in society. They don't understand that another person's suffering and happiness is linked to their own. When children don't have a good education and lack skills, their self-esteem plummets. When they become teenagers and adults, they turn to drugs and alcohol to medicate their pain. Children who don't have the opportunity to engage in constructive activities after school – sports, dancing, art, music, and so forth – are alone in their homes or more likely, on the streets, and trouble results: drug and alcohol use, weapons, gang activity. Whose houses do they vandalize to get money or to prove their power? The homes of the very people who refused to pay more taxes to support schools, childcare, extracurricular activities at schools and community centers! This happens because we are inter-related. What happens to other people's children affects all of us. If we live in a society with miserable people, we have problems too. Therefore, we have to take care of everyone. As H.H. Dalai Lama says, "If you want to be selfish, do so by taking care of others." In other words, since we influence each other, to be happy ourselves, we have to help those around us. When we live with others who are happy, we have fewer problems; when we live with people who are miserable, their misery affects us.

Drug and alcohol abuse isn't a problem just in poor communities; it's just that it is easier to arrest the poor because more of their community life occurs outdoors on the streets and because the police focus on those areas of a city. Domestic violence, substance abuse, and children feeling unloved are problems in middle-class and wealthy families as well. Sometimes the parents in those families are so busy working to earn money to get their children more possessions that they have little time to spend being with, and talking to, their children.

In addition, people are unwilling to acknowledge that their behavior plays a role in family members abusing drugs and alcohol. The people who tell their children, "Don't drink and drug just because your friends do. Don't give in to peer pressure; just say no when they ask," are the same people who succumb to peer pressure themselves. These adults do things because their friends are doing it. They say, "I have to go out with business clients and have a drink when we discuss business arrangements. I won't be able to close the deal otherwise." Or they say, "My friends drink so when they invite me to parties, I must too. Otherwise, they will think badly of me. Some lay Buddhists say, "If I don't drink, they'll think I'm a prude and will think badly of Buddhism. So I drink with them so that they won't criticize Buddhism." This is a rubbish excuse!

Robert: I have had the opportunity to work with some youth programs locally. The programs have been for kids in some dire circumstances who have got themselves in trouble with the law. Invariably, we end up talking about the DARE program (Drug Abuse Resistance Education), which by all accounts is a dismal failure. I tell these kids that DARE is not to keep kids off drugs as much as it is to keep parents off Martinis and Prozac. The parents are role models for their children. The parents drink or drug in order to relax; they need *something* to cope with stress and turn to alcohol and drugs. But, when their kids feel unhappy or confused, these same parents can't offer constructive advice and instead tell their kids to endure those feelings. In the end, the children do just what their parents do. Rather than go to the liquor store or ask their friend the physician for a prescription, the kids go to their dealer. So we are really looking at the issue of parenting and modeling.

Ven. Chodron: Yes.

Robert: I would like to touch on the subject of the environment before we close.

Ven. Chodron: I feel very strongly about that. At least two Buddhist principles prompt us to awareness about the importance of caring for the environment. The two I'm thinking of are, firstly, compassion, and the second is interdependence. One attitude that lies behind environmental pollution is the greed to have more and better. Another is the apathy that says, "If it won't happen until I'm dead, why should I care?" Both of these are antithetical to compassion. Compassion for sentient beings is an essential principle in all Buddhist traditions. If we truly care about other living beings, we have to care about the environment that they live in. Why? Because sentient beings live in an environment, and if that environment is not healthy, they will not be able to survive. These sentient beings of the future may be your children and grandchildren, or they may be you in your future lives. If we care about them, we can't leave them a devastated environment to live in.

In addition, we live in an interdependent world, not only dependent upon other living beings but also upon our shared environment. This means that we must care about the planet as a whole, not just the area where we live. It also means that we have a personal responsibility to protect the environment. It's not just large corporations or government policies that affect the environment; our individual actions are involved as well. The individual is related to the whole and the whole to the individual.

As individuals, we can act to preserve the environment. If we cultivate an expanded world-view, then helping sentient beings and protecting their environment are not difficult. For example, we want the newest computers, cell phones, cars, clothes, sports equipment, and so on. Do we really need these to be happy? Producing so many goods and disposing of them later after they are obsolete (even though they still function perfectly well), harms our shared environment. As Americans, we use a disproportionate amount of the world's natural resources by consuming things that we really don't need and that don't make us truly happy. This is not to mention the amount of resources consumed to fight wars or sold to others involved in warfare. Of course, other countries will not be pleased with us for this. Why are we so surprised that other peoples are not fond of us when we are acting in such self-centered ways?

We don't really need for everyone in the family to have their own TV or their own computer or their own car. What about using public transportation or carpooling? Walking or cycling to nearby destinations will improve our health. But it's hard for us to relinquish the attitude, "I want freedom to get into my car and go where I want to go when I want to go there." What would happen if, when we got into the car, we asked ourselves, "Where am I going and why am I going there? Will that bring happiness to me and to other living beings?" Just pausing for a moment before zooming off, we may discover that we don't really need to go to all of the places we think we need to go. In fact, we may even be less stressed and have better family relationships if we aren't so busy going here and there.

Robert: Along with this sense of individual responsibility at the local level, how do you think individuals can most effectively make efforts to influence large structures and institutions such as governments and corporations?

Ven. Chodron: Recycling and reducing waste are extremely important, but even the most well-meaning people sometimes neglect these. For example, once I was having lunch with a husband and wife who were both professors of ecology at a university. They cared very much about the environment and encouraged government leaders to adopt policies that benefit the environment. One day, one of their kids came home from school and said, "Why aren't we recycling? It helps the environment." The parents told me that they had never thought of that before, but because their child reminded them they started doing it.

Robert: Finally, Venerable, many of the teachers have spoken about some of the difficulties we may be facing in the immediate future. So, after speaking about war, environmental issues, and so on, if you were to look at the next 100 years, what do you see? Which issues would be most easily solved and which ones do you think will persist?

Ven. Chodron: To be honest, I don't find that kind of question very useful. My opinion about what could happen in the next 100 years doesn't make a difference. It doesn't improve the situation. Spending my mental energy thinking about the next 100 years is a waste of my mental energy. Even if I did put my energy there and developed an opinion, I don't think that opinion would be very useful for anybody.

What is important is cultivating a kind heart right now. Forget the next 100 years. Right now, we need to emphasize the importance of training our minds to see the goodness in other people and generating a kind, patient, tolerant heart inside of ourselves. Your first question was about a "degenerate age," and your subsequent questions concerned war, sickness, and poverty. Underlying all of these questions is the assumption that everything is falling apart, that there is no human goodness, that we and the world are doomed.

I don't accept that world-view. It's unbalanced, discourages us from taking positive action that could be helpful, and becomes a self-fulfilling prophesy. There are many problems – we are in samsara so we must expect that. But there is a lot of goodness and we need to pay attention to the goodness in other people and the goodness in ourselves and to put more energy and time into cultivating it. That needs to be done right now. If we do that now, we don't need to worry about what life will be like 100 years from now.

Robert: I remember once speaking with an American female meditator by the name of Karma Wangmo. I brought up the idea of the dark age and she thought that, in fact, people were actually more aware and compassionate. Due to the immediacy of mass communication, we hear of all the wars and problems around us. Could it be that those have always been there, but we no longer hide or deny their presence? We not only know what is happening in our own town, but we hear what is going on elsewhere, and it has an impact on us. And, because of this, we are now trying to do something about it.

Ven. Chodron: Human beings have always had ignorance, anger, and attachment. We know more about each others' lives and environments due to telecommunications. That there are conflicts between human beings is nothing new, even though weapons used are more sophisticated. Suffering in samsara is age-old.

Robert: Counter-culture movements – be they the anti-war or environmental groups – often confront the situation and those who they perceive as the main perpetrators with an "anti" position. When their objectives are not achieved they become demoralized and subsequently slide into ignoring the situation. Those whose hearts are still in the "struggle" get depressed. What advice would you give people to encourage them to be part of the solution to some of the problems we have been discussing? What would be your parting word to them?

Ven. Chodron: First, it's important to have a long-term view and purpose. Having an idealistic hope for quick change is a set-up for discouragement. But if we cultivate inner strength, we can act compassionately and consistently for as long as it takes to bring about good results.

Second, stop thinking that you, as one individual, can change everything and solve all problems. We are not that powerful. Of course, we can make a worthwhile and powerful contribution, but we cannot control what other people do. We cannot control all the various conditions that affect the world.

Third, do not get depressed because you can't effect quick change and solve all the problems in the world. No matter how wonderful it would be to be able to do this, it is an unrealistic belief. What we need to do is to become much more realistic. We are all individuals and we have the responsibility of an individual. Thus we must think: What can I do within my capabilities? I certainly can't do things that I am incapable of doing or don't have the skill to do, so there's no sense in being dejected by that. But I can act within my capabilities, so I must consider how to use my abilities in an effective way to benefit others. In addition, I have to think about how to act consistently over time, without going up and down a lot. In other words, we each act according to our own individual abilities and, at the same time, work to increase what we are capable of doing. By this, I don't just mean necessarily typing ability or computer ability. I also mean internal abilities, such as developing compassion.

Let's pull ourselves out of this all-or-nothing attitude, this attitude that says that I should be able to change everything or I get depressed because change doesn't happen quickly. Let's have a long-term perspective and take one step at a time, cultivating our good qualities and abilities, and influencing others in a constructive way so that we can contribute over a long period of time. To me, that is what the bodhisattva path is about. When you follow the bodhisattva path, you have to be willing to hang in there with sentient beings for eons and eons and eons, no matter how they treat you and no matter how much they do things that sabotage their own happiness. Buddhas and bodhisattvas are hanging in with us too, no matter how obnoxious we are. Isn't that wonderful? Where would we be if they gave up on us because we keep doing the opposite of what is good for us? We have to cultivate compassion like theirs, compassion that can bear anything without discouragement, compassion that keeps helping no matter what.

From the Buddhist perspective, ignorance that misapprehends reality is the source of all our problems. This ignorance can be counteracted because it is mistaken. As we develop the wisdom that knows things as they are, it eliminates this ignorance. Without ignorance as their support, all the mental afflictions, such as greed, resentment, and so on, crumble. Without the mental afflictions that motivate destructive actions, such actions cease. With this comes the cessation of suffering.

Here we see that suffering isn't really necessary. It isn't a given. It has a cause. If we can remove the cause then the suffering results are eliminated. So that allows for an optimistic perspective with which we can move forward.

Ignorance and suffering can be eliminated. Can this be done quickly? No, because we have a lot of conditioning behind us. We have a lot of bad habits, some of which we're not even aware we have. But, it doesn't matter how long it takes to eliminate them, because the direction we are going in is a good direction. If we don't go in that direction, what are we going to do? The only alternative is to have a "pity party," but that's not much fun, and self-pity is of no benefit at all. So, you do what you can, what you are capable of, with a happy mind going in a positive direction no matter how long it takes. You find joy and satisfaction in the doing of whatever you are capable of doing. In other words, be more concerned with the process of what you are doing than with attaining a specific result that is part of your agenda.

Robert: Before closing, I have a practical question about the current debacle of the US with the Middle East. How do you see this conflict most quickly coming to resolution?

Ven. Chodron: I have no idea. I cannot give you a quick, practical prognosis.

Robert: Well then, what are the elements that are important for a solution?

Ven. Chodron: What is needed is respect for every human being. People need to trust each other. That, I think, is the most difficult point in the Middle East conflict right now. The Israelis and Palestinians don't trust each other. The Shiites, Sunnis, and Americans don't trust each other. When you don't trust others, then everything the other person does you see in a bad light. When there is a lot of hurt, pain, and violence, trust becomes difficult.

I heard about a program called "Seeds of Change" which took kids from areas of conflict and got them together in a summer camp in New England. There they met actual human beings – kids their own age who were on the other side of the conflict that they were all caught in the middle of. This personal contact allowed for some empathy and trust to grow. How to accomplish this when millions of people are involved, I don't know. So I start with myself and try to cultivate forgiveness and trust. It's hard enough to release my individual personal grudges; on a group level, doing so is much more difficult. But we keep trying.

Robert: Thank you so much, Venerable.

Christopher Titmuss

ABOUT CHRISTOPHER TITMUSS

Christopher Titmuss, a former Buddhist monk in Thailand and India, teaches awakening and insight meditation around the world. He is the founder and director of the Dharma Facilitators Programme and the Living Dharma Programme, an online mentor program for dharma practitioners. He gives retreats, participates in pilgrimages (*yatras*), and leads dharma gatherings. Christopher has been teaching annual retreats in Bodh Gaya, India since 1975 and has led an annual Dharma Gathering in Sarnath since 1999.

A senior dharma teacher in the West, he is the author of numerous books including *Light on Enlightenment, An Awakened Life,* and *Transforming Our Terror.* A campaigner for peace and other global issues, Christopher is a member of the international advisory council of the Buddhist Peace Fellowship. Poet and writer, he is the co-founder of Gaia House, an international retreat centre in Devon, England. He lives in Totnes, Devon, England.

In America, Christopher Titmuss is most well known through the Insight Meditation community, whose main center on the West Coast is Spirit Rock near San Francisco. It was through a friend close to that community that I heard of him and his work. Once I had discovered how socially and politically active he was, it would have been remiss not to have included Christopher in this book.

Initially I googled Christopher to find out exactly where he was. So, it was like making a cold call and I really did not know whether I would get through or not. After several tries, I did reach him and we set a time and date. Like several of the interviews, this one needed to be long distance with me at home and Christopher likewise at home in Devon. It took place in the fall of 2006. Christopher is very thorough; philosophical, yet absolutely to the point. I felt that I was engaging a teacher and, at the same time, a new friend.

THE INTERVIEW

Robert: In looking at the interview questionnaire, you commented that you wanted to focus on global issues, especially war, terror by states, and religious fundamentalism...

Christopher: Certainly I also include the problems of nation-states. We live in the time of "the American Empire." We are also making war on the environment including the resources of land, water, and air.

Robert: I have spoken with many teachers about the notion of a dark age. I would like to hear your perspective on this.

Christopher: I think in the strictest terms the notion of a dark age comes from the Hindu concept of the Kali Yuga. I suspect that people of generation after generation have thought of themselves living in apocalyptic times. Whether this period is any darker than any other time however... If we go back to the last century we can reflect on all of what took place then around the world; 50 million people dying in

World War II for example. Rather than calling our period a darker age, scientific evidence shows that the period we live in is critical, simply because of the impact human behavior is having on Mother Earth and her resources. The weight of the evidence suggests that we have to change our behavior in a variety of ways. If we just draw a conclusion that we are in a dark age, then it could carry despair, negativity, a degree of helplessness, and a picture that is fatalistic. So I prefer to keep out "dark age" partly because it is a conclusion and partly because it is a despairing generalized view.

Robert: So whilst there have always been sickness and poverty, the most critical aspect is the sheer impact of humanity on the earth itself.

Christopher: Yes.

Robert: So let us start there. How do you think we are impacting this earth?

Christopher: There are certainly three major ways that we have an impact on the earth.

The first major area is warfare and the conventional weapons of mass destruction. For example, in the UK where I live, for about every pound we pay in tax, 27 pence – or a bit more than a quarter of it – goes to supporting defense; our government has recently announced new contracts for nuclear programs for a billion pounds, new military helicopters, etc. We make war. A few figures here: Since AD 900, the English have been engaged in more wars than any other nation on earth; 56 years out of every 100. This island is a warmongering island. And it still continues currently as we stand with the Americans in the war on the people of Iraq and Afghanistan. America has invaded 19 countries in the past 50 years, as well as engineered numerous military coups, the destruction of democracies, etc. There is so-called 'war on terror' – against extremism in Islam in the Arab world. The cost to people's lives, including the psychological cost, and to the environment is a nightmare. It's horrendous.

The second major area is the corporate world and the destructive impact the primary corporations have on this world. The very top corporations in the world include Marlboro cigarettes, Coca-Cola, Google (which supported censorship to satisfy Chinese authorities. Type in "Abuse of human rights in China" and up will come Chinese government websites), MacDonalds, Nike (it costs $1 to make a pair of trainers in Indonesian factories), Wal-Mart (employs 185,000 workers in dreadful conditions in clothing factories in China). In India, every can of Coca-Cola produced requires ten times the amount of water to make that one can. There are eight spoons of sugar in a can. So beyond the nuclear arms trade, the global impact on resources by these companies is horrendous.

Then the third primary area is – of course – consumers. If everybody lived like people in the Bay Area, it would take at least six planets to support us all. We read that 52 percent of the vehicles now in the United States are SUVs. This is one small example.

So all these three – our consumption, corporate control over resources or globalization in the corporate world, the arms trade and war – have a tremendous impact. The dharma and the Four Noble Truths have to be used as a vehicle or means to challenge all of these areas.

Robert: So the idea here is to take the wisdom and compassion at the core of Buddhist teachings and apply it in very practical ways to address these issues.

Christopher: If these are not going directly into practical areas, then all of it is a navel-gazing club.

Robert: I used to talk about "enlightenment from the neck up…" [Laughter.]

I think it is interesting that today (early July 2006) for seemingly the first time on a major television network, there is some serious discussion about global warming. I imagine that this has to do with the recent release of Al Gore's film, *An Inconvenient Truth*. I wanted to know how you see this problem.

Christopher: I think that "global warming" is a much over-used term. I think what we are actually talking about, more significantly, is climate change. I was flying into Dusseldorf, Germany, just a few days ago. As we were coming in to land there were these huge concrete towers emitting massive amounts of pollution into the air. I saw the amount of pollution that was pouring out of the backs of the airplanes. So I should take as much responsibility as anyone else in terms of diluted resources. So, apart from challenging the powers that be, as part of a committed activity, we also have to do a great deal of soul searching as well and really ask ourselves, "What can I do without? What can I live without? Where can I take care and attention to a mindful life?" It is meeting the way of both the inner life, desire basically, and the outer life, to ask what our leaders and representatives are doing and what is going on in the boardrooms of big business that affects our lives and affects our planet. This inner and outer dialogue is significant and vital.

Robert: I think that the harsh reality is that often disaster is the best teacher; that we have wisdom traditions that point to these things and people pay lip service to them until finally something really does happen. But it seems that we are at a point globally where we are teetering on one of those brinks that we certainly don't want to go over.

Christopher: Unfortunately, for numerous people around the world, disasters are already happening. In terms of the impact on people's lives one thinks of tsunamis, the hurricanes that struck the southern coast of the United States, and the other earthquakes, floods, famines, the gradual destruction in sub-Saharan Africa; the war in the Middle East – the punishment of the Palestinian community, the 100,000 deaths of civilians in Iraq, etc. These have to be addressed by you and me and others. We don't have to wait for major impending disasters. These are already major disasters for people.

Somehow, in the madness of consumer culture we have become modern, living in debt. A sad and major consequence is that there is a dreadful numbing effect on people. To give a small example, I go to Israel twice a year since the early 1990s. It is barely possible to mention the word "peace" in Israel or Palestine. It is a nightmare for both communities, but especially the Palestinians, who, as a people, suffer far, far more than the Israelis. Thoughtful citizens in the region are sick to death of promises and broken promises and having it in their face, day in and day out. In Israel, the key word is "security" rather than "justice" or "reconciliation" or "respect for the rights of people." This is just one small example. We are overloaded with information – even though we all have a sense that something is not right on the earth.

There are great communities of people, NGO organizations, anti-globalization organizations, environmental movements that campaign for people, land, water, and air. Such people who work for such organizations are our guardian angels. We certainly need more voices.

Robert: So in some ways, getting back to your example of Israel and the Palestinians, "peace" almost becomes a dirty word or it seems benign or insignificant compared to the actual right to survive.

Christopher: Yes, exactly. I am sure that what the Palestinians feel is much the same as the Iraqi community feels about the terrible conflict there, and the Afghan community, and elsewhere in the world. It is an enormous task to just get through the day and tend to your family, your loved ones, your community, and their survival. This will always be the case when people are oppressed. Sadly, there is a pathological sickness in Western societies. There is a fanatical determination to impose our horrendous value system on other parts of the world – the two-party state, corporate ownership of resources, and the conversion of people into consumers of those resources – this is the "triple gem" of the West. The West is brutally determined to make sure that others conform to this system of behaviour. This has sweeping consequences for those who don't wish to live that way of life. And certainly the Islamic world is not going to compromise, not going to succumb to it.

In Britain and the United States, democracy is a fiction. In Britain, only one in five, exactly 20 percent of the people who are eligible to vote, actually voted in the British government. Eighty percent did not vote for it. Yet it has an overwhelming majority as if it were a one-party state. And only 35 percent of the voters actually voted for this government. Ruled by the majority? It's a fiction. The same is true in the United States.

Robert: In some ways it is no different than the 99 percent who voted for Saddam Hussein in Iraq.

Christopher: Exactly. There are some rather sad parallels in that, of course, Saddam Hussein executed his citizens, but George Bush, as the governor of Texas, ordered the execution of 150 of its citizens. There are sickening parallels. When the West points its accusatory finger at some other ugly regimes in the world, it should remember that it has the other three fingers pointing at itself.

Robert: Yes, that is always a good image to give people about pointing at others. In this way, Christopher, obviously you have the reality of corporatism around the world and you speak of the materialistic "triple gem" of the West. Where do you see the place of fundamentalism in this scheme? Obviously, wars and takeovers of various kinds have been justified in religious terms. How do the three aspects of the "triple gem" and fundamentalism interact and mutually feed upon each other?

Christopher: I think this is a major area worth exploring. There are two or three features of this. One is, putting it in a very simple way, that monotheism – particularly the Middle Eastern brand of it – really has to look at the intensity of its identification with its belief system – and I've got in mind here Judaism, Islam, and Christianity. All three are sons of the patriarch, Abraham – a three-branch off from that root, we could say – yet the intensity and the distances and divisions within each, ranging from the progressives to the orthodox, the ultra-orthodox and the ultra-ultra-orthodox has not only religious impact, but also social and political ones. That would be one area. There is growing extremism in religion in India, despite a history of tolerance. Religion and the identification of certain religious people with their belief systems do generate conflict. It has to.

Another issue which goes along with this is the identification with the nation-state. This is a severe problem. Take these two together and you have a dangerous mixture, not only for those people who identify the two together, but also from those who advocate the superiority of their religion for a whole variety of reasons. I mention these three religions because in traveling around this world, beyond my connection to Hinduism and Buddhism, I have quite a degree of connection with, and get to see the effects of, these three faiths.

Robert: What seems ironic is that in this modern age, we have virtually made obsolete the concept of nation-state through transportation, communication, and global commerce. Similarly, now being exposed to more faiths and other cultures than ever before, it is far more tenuous to even to consider one's own faith as the only option in looking at cultural, social, or existential issues. As we bump up against other cultures and the ensuing globalism, so much of what we held as true and/or identified with, as citizens of an identifiable entity or member of one flock, has become blurry. And for some, it would seem a formula for encouraging more xenophobia, nationalism, and fundamentalism.

Christopher: It is true. But also, in fact – in the face of this – little has changed in a certain way. For example, we read here in Europe that only 10 percent of US citizens have passports. And therefore the amount of actual international travel – getting out of North America – by American citizens is tragically low. So American citizens tend to have a rather small, parochial, and insular world-view. When I come to the US, New York City and the Bay Area – supposed to be more "enlightened" than other parts of the United States – when I pick up the newspapers and look at the *New York Times* or the *San Francisco Chronicle* – these are incredibly lightweight newspapers – and I watch news programs punctuated with all of the commercials, it is not surprising that US citizens have little clue as to what is going on in the world. US citizens fear to appear to be unpatriotic – even among relatively enlightened people. Though one might get a clip on the news of a differing view from the US from the so-called democratic media, these clips are so short. Instead of creating a healthy cynicism, the deference that your media pay to your leaders is so strong that, unfortunately, there is really little opportunity for the US citizens to have any clear view of what is going on. There is not a vigorous or vibrant debate in the daily press of the US.

Robert: In fall of 2002, before the invasion in Iraq, Melanie and I were in Europe. We were watching the news and reading what we could in both Germany and England about what was happening with American troop deployments – aircraft carriers heading to surround Iraq. The media was bracing everyone for war. Then, we returned to the US and were asking people about the troops and the plans and the impending war.

Strangely for us, no one knew what we were talking about. There was a literal media blackout of this information. When I was invited to come on one of the local talk-radio shows, not only did people think I was exaggerating, they also were very questioning of my patriotism.

Christopher: Exactly. So you know this is true from your own experience. Sadly, this is all obscured and hidden from the rhetoric of a free society and freedom of the press. Being an old newspaper reporter myself from times past, it is part of the contemporary mythology. The owners of the media are too close to the rest of the corporate world and the government of the day. Al Gore wrote *Earth in the Balance* before his election as vice president and right after the Rio Summit. He was in office for eight years. Did we hear anything after that? Was there any real challenge to the corporate world? Was there a slowing down of the American economy? Or was there a tremendous encouragement for economic growth? Out of office, suddenly both Clinton and Gore are beginning to talk about the fate of the earth. Perhaps significant change takes place outside of democracy, out of the normal political sphere and in the grass-roots organizations and networks. We have put our faith in such organizations.

Robert: So, I guess you are saying, on a positive note, that you do not have much confidence that the government structures in these Western states will necessarily make changes unless there is a strong prompting from grass-roots organizations.

Christopher: I think that in a dualistic view (using a dharma term) the challenge of the times we live in is that the demand for responsibility and accountability from our governments will come from outside of government. We, who are in the protest movement, the global change movement, anti-globalization movement, find ourselves increasingly, in the last 10 to 20 years, challenging governments and the corporate world equally because the corporate world has such a controlling influence over government policy and, of course, directly and indirectly, is funding government policy. So, our political masters tend to be working alongside the corporate world.

Robert: You are probably more in touch with the Buddhist community of both Britain and Europe. How much do you see Buddhists participating in these grass-roots movements?

Christopher: I am an international dharma teacher. It takes me to four continents every year. That means Europe, Asia, Israel/Palestine, India, Australia, and the USA. This gives me the opportunity to listen a lot, speak a lot of course, and to have some sense of the international contemporary Buddhist world. To some degree, there is some movement and change taking place in the Western dharma world. First, increasingly, Westerners are willing to leave behind in the East a lot of the medieval religious stuff of Buddhism; to squeeze the honey out of the religion which is mainly the dharma and its practices. So, the religion of Buddhism is more and more low-profile, and what Westerners are saying is that we want something down to earth, practical, that can be implemented into daily life. As a small example, the range of themes which appeal in the West would certainly be:

- ◆ a Buddhist nonviolent approach to life,
- ◆ care for people, animals, and environment – a kind of core theme in the best of the traditions,
- ◆ an emphasis on kindness and compassion,
- ◆ the current dharma word in the psychotherapy/psychology world of "mindfulness," which has hit a chord with people in dealing with some of the various degrees of mental health and stress,
- ◆ the emphasis on right livelihood rather than career,
- ◆ the exploration of what suffering is and its resolution,

◆ the interdependency (rather than the interconnectedness) that we all have on each other and the earth.

So these threads and themes and the deep meditations of insight meditation, the discipline of Zen, these touch deep places with people and offer something profoundly important and in stark contrast to religion and its belief systems, whether it is in the guru, the savior, the prophet, the lineage, the Book (the dreaded "Book") or whatever. But, having said that, with respect to my appreciation for the best of what the dharma has to offer, i.e. the Four Noble Truths and its resolute exploration into daily life, the vulnerability of Buddhism has been its inadequate response to global issues, period. There are some great and fine exceptions, but in a general way, it is apolitical rather than political.

Robert: An interesting aspect of this for me personally came when I had my own "wake-up" with respect to politics after the US presidential election in 2000, becoming more amplified after the 2004 election. During that time I wrote the book *The Buddha at War*, and there were a few of my Buddhist friends who definitely wanted me to change the title. I did not want to and this did not please them. I then went to a number of American publishers who specialized in this field and was told that I did not have enough popular draw or a platform for them to justify the economic risk of publishing my book. They also did not think that most spiritually minded people would stay that focused on some of the issues I brought out, and that certainly after the 2004 US presidential election, no one was really going to be paying attention to politics all that much. Fortunately, I contacted Michael Mann of Watkins in the UK who I was familiar with, and he eagerly accepted it. I think that Europeans are a little more jaded about their media, don't idealize or romanticize about religion, and have more savvy

about the political realities in the world. But here, in the US, I
think in some sectors of the Western Buddhist community
there is the unfortunate view that your meditation, your
spiritual practice and life should be separate and not somehow
connected to these social and political realities. It's like a
benign compassion and wisdom with no hands.

Christopher: Exactly. And unfortunately in the Buddhist world, there
are some historical shadows. I think that this shadow is rather uncon-
scious. Having been a Buddhist monk for six years in the monasteries,
the forests and the caves, it is in a sense, an other-worldly activity. I had
no idea from one month or one year what was going on in the world
and it was just not even on the periphery of my consciousness as a
meditator. I think it is very important that that way of life is supported
and protected. But there is a bit of shadow with so much emphasis on
non-attachment, not being identified with, and a common view that
runs through Buddhism that has led to some of the most intolerant
regimes in the East.

Political action coming from the standpoint of the Four Noble
Truths has nothing to do with supporting the nation-state, it is not
about party politics, but is a way of being that is engaged in the world
as it is. Party politics belongs to the past. Authentic politics is grass-roots
engagement and that is not an easy culture or climate to move in; where
there is a commitment to be well informed and to take what steps we
see are necessary. US Buddhists generally take little interest in renunciation – the giving up of desires for material things, position and
status. US Buddhists can learn a lot from the Euro-Buddhist tradition
in this area. There is a great army of people in the medical profession,
the teaching profession, psychologists, psychotherapists, people who are
involved in retreat centers – this army is doing important and
wonderful work and is a backbone of effort to keep people's lives at least
relatively sane amidst our madness. I give a lot of credit to the people
who engage in this. But we need an army of people, as well, who are

neither afraid nor shy of taking on the big global issues. People on their own will get crushed by the scale of the problems. But, together, we make change. I have said to people in my travels, valuable changes have taken place in the world because a few people sat around on a few chairs in somebody's home one evening and literally said, "Something has to be done." That is how things start. I would like to see more of the army of dharma practitioners working to change the oppressive system that we live under and countless others elsewhere. There are some wonderful voices, but this number is relatively small.

Robert: Which high-profile Buddhist leaders do you see most engaged in social and political change at this time?

Christopher: There are obvious Asian names that stick out: the Dalai Lama in his dual role as religious and political leader, Dr Ariyaratne, Aung San Suu Kyi – she is a pillar, another great voice – and Sulak Sivaraksa, the Thai dissident who has just written a book called *Socially Engaged Buddhism*. We have to find skillful ways and means and those of us who are privileged to be dharma teachers have to bring in the global much more than just being basically meditation teachers. Once one engages the larger dimensions of human life, then we are going to tread on the toes of those who desire to control and exploit people and resources. In America, because there is a division between religion and politics, I get notes from people saying, "We came here to learn meditation, not be lectured on global issues." Religion, politics, and science are human constructs and have to be challenged. That's the purpose of dharma – to liberate us from such constructs – by engagement, not avoidance.

Robert: I have had the same experience.

Chistopher: Unfortunately, in the Buddhist tradition, there is fear amongst Buddhists of appearing judgmental. There is a confusion in the tradition, I feel, between being judgmental, laying blame, negativity and putting down, and criticism. Criticism is looking at something, seeing it as clearly as we possibly can, and offering as much of a view based on understanding and resolution. Being judgmental is just dumping our shadows and negativities on organizations or groups or governments or the corporate world. Frankly, Buddhists want to appear to be nice and thus are ineffectual.

Robert: If you were to look down the road, for the next 50 to 60 years, at these grass-roots movements alongside the intractability of some of the government and corporate structures, and the holding onto the notion of the nation-state, where do you see things moving?

Christopher: I think, from a dharma viewpoint, we have an essential vision already that – to keep it simple and in accordance with the Four Noble Truths:

1 There is suffering in this world. This has to be understood.
2 There are causes and conditions for suffering. These causes and conditions have to change, to be allowed to go.
3 There is liberation, a total revolution.
4 There are ways, called "the path" to do it, that have to be developed and along with this, some understanding of the "dependent arising of conditions" – a critically key concept. To understand the dharma you need to understand dependent arising. We need to explore the relationship of dependent arising conditions and this web of life.

So the way we have to go is to look at the causes and conditions for suffering – personally, socially, politically, economically, globally. Secondly, we need to free ourselves from the nightmare of the nation-state and explore the dependently arising conditions – a sense of interdependence combined with the way we all influence each other.

Thirdly, we have to look at all the dualities, especially the core problematic duality which can be "I and you" or "us and them" and mix these into our personal lives. If we work to remove this at a personal level, and the conflicts and tension that go with it, we can aim to dissolve the "us and them" issues on the international level. This is a small earth. We are all in it together. You and I have to change the vision. That, to me, is the liberating and awakening direction we need to speak about. Because the current method, the current psychology, the current conditioning is destructive.

Robert: So, you are speaking of a potential that is there and offering the steps that we need to take to meet that potential.

Christopher: Absolutely. And I think that Buddhism, with the emphasis on the "ism," is somewhat of an irrelevant factor in all of this. I think that the Buddha would not blink an eyelid if he attended the cremation of Buddhism.

Robert: Interesting…

Christopher: I think we have to lower dramatically the temperature of religion and also question science. In the West, we moved out of the medieval religious beliefs, i.e. God created the world and God imposed rewards and punishments for human behavior. Then in came the Age of, so-called, "Enlightenment," the age of science making a shift away from these beliefs into faith in reason, the supremacy of thought, and the world of technology. What science has lacked is a profound ethic to go with this huge skill we have to use our minds, to make and create. Hence, two thirds of scientists work for the military research. There is growing doubt in the promises of a century ago that science and rationality would answer all of our prayers. This is now proved to be another myth. So we need to draw out what is best in science and religion, the mind and the heart to serve one and all. We need to draw the best from natural wisdom. We are not going to throw out religion. We are not going to throw out science. Science and religion serve different inner needs. The arrogance of both scientists and religionists is the claim to know what true reality is.

Robert: I think what you are advising is not only the elimination of the notion of the nation-state, but also essentially the morality that sets up the dual self and worse still, self versus other.

Christopher: Exactly. In the nature of things, when we are touching deeper places from a liberated perspective, there is no self-other in reality. The "other" is a movement of the inner life which projects itself onto people and invests so-called "others" with various characteristics which are different from one's self. This legitimizes good and evil, us and them. "They" engage in doing this in exactly the same way as us. So this self-other duality feeds hate, war, conflict, marital breakdown, disputes, tension, and a lack of communication.

As I said, when I meet with Israelis or Palestinians, the only way there can be any real meeting is when we hold very lightly the identity "I am a Jew" or "I am a Muslim," "I am an Israeli" or "I am a Palestinian." Then we hold respect for the culture, respect for the label, but then you have got to dig deeper and look at the shared humanity. It is not a question to stop being a Muslim or Jew or stop being a Palestinian or Israeli. If identity is held strongly, it will produce the "other." We have to realize a non-dual base; the dharma teaching of having a keen interest in this non-dual exploration, beyond "I, me, and mine," "I and you" – the torment, stress, and terror of humanity.

Robert: It almost sounds like you are even talking about a very significant evolutionary step. If we look at Buddhism from the standpoint of its being, in the purest sense, a mind science, perhaps up until this modern scientific time, it has

been the religious cloak of Buddhism that has carried forth the
ideas of the interconnectedness of all life and so on. But, with
the methods now available in science which prove these ideas,
the fact that Buddha's teachings have been labeled as an
"ism"over time is now more of a barrier than a benefit.

Christopher: True. I find myself a little hesitant with our Western
language when you talk about an "evolutionary" or "pure" science. I
would rather take the view of the more immediate, radical, fresh
understanding in the moment which then influences and gives shape
to our actions – if you see what I mean – rather than in the future or
making evolutionary steps. It is a radical seeing that is not spellbound
by technology and therefore neither a slave to it, nor spellbound by
religion and its dreadful tendency to moralize. We must find a clear
wisdom and realization about the nature of life, not shaped by the
dogma of science or religion, but at the same time not be so stupid as
to reject them both.

Robert: I have been able to speak with Ajahn Amaro. From
Theravadin cosmology, he said that we are in a dark age, but
currently in a 100-year "grace period" at the beginning of the
time of the abyss where there is a phenomenal amount of
growth and the kind of knowledge that you are describing is
available. Roshi Joan Halifax spoke of this cyber-sangha – if
you will – a web that is growing all over this planet via the kind
of technology we are using to do this interview (i.e. the
Internet). Ajahn Amaro said that after this 100-year period, the
opportunity for such growth and development would
diminish. I also spoke, years ago, with a Tibetan Buddhist
teacher by the name of Namgyal Rinpoche who I met in the
UK in the late 1970s who did not have much confidence that
the Aquarian Age was going to be a time of great
progressiveness. He suggested that the ideas you are describing

would be held by small communities, what he called "pockets of light" in a very dark world; a world that was dominated by massive bureaucratization and institutionalization – in some ways not dissimilar to what you have been mentioning with respect to corporations. But it was very important to keep this dialogue going in terms of personal growth, and also on all levels – at the same time realizing that these ideas would not become the dominant paradigm of the time.

Like yourself, I see that those who subscribe to Buddhism or Buddhist principles are more focused on health, healing, and personal transformation, with few being willing to step out into the world of social and political activism and reform to take on the macro issues that are facing us. All that said, how do you see the development of the conscious community actually happening?

Christopher: I hesitate to speculate about the future. I respect the time-honored tradition of the Buddha in not speculating about how things will be in the future. Will human beings exist in the future or not? Our views are fueled by how we are feeling today. If we are in a good mood today, we have a good feeling about the future. If things are difficult, then we have a more pessimistic view. Some days we think, there are 6 billion people on the earth and its pretty amazing how well life is going on. Considering the number of wars, there are far fewer people in the middle of a war and many are free from the curse of it. For example, the barbarism of Europe has changed dramatically in the last two generations. So one can look one way and some could look at it another way.

Middle-class Buddhists use terms like "interconnectedness" that produce a spiritual feeling. These terms mean nothing to people who are really suffering. People who are just trying to get by and survive in the villages of Asia, in a war zone of Africa. When they don't have relevance they become a dogma – a pleasing, pleasant dogma, but it is just another ideology. Dependent arising isn't sweet language. We have to look at what is dependently arising and will change what is. We have to keep questioning about our views, our dogmas, and our metaphors, and our time-ridden perception called past, present, and future.

We're not just settling in for some middle-class spiritual views masquerading as reality. We have to see the emptiness of all of our mental constructions and not one of them – even the pleasant ones – is worth clinging to – so that we have a genuine liberated sense of our being. Love is still the powerful force in this world. Unfortunately, the Buddhist world has watered down the term "metta" or "love" into nice feelings of sending nice positive loving-kindness messages.

Robert: Nice fluffy pillows...

Christopher: Exactly – fluffy pillows for fluffy minds. Love is a powerful force and gains tremendous power when we are not tied to ideology; religious, scientific, nation-state or whatever.

Robert: As we are winding down, Christopher, my hope for this book is that it is not just read by middle-class Buddhists. I want to see this go to places where there are levels of suffering that do demand immediate attention. In that regard – what direct encouragement would you give to people in those circumstances?

Christopher: Where there is suffering, we need to use "skillful means." We do not rely on absolute truth statements nor make fictional promises for the future. We have to take risks. What are the questions we need to ask? What challenges us? Who do we need to listen to? Supported with liberated realizations, the power of "metta," the power of love, the power of compassion finds a way through these nightmares.

Tenzin Robert Thurman

ABOUT TENZIN ROBERT THURMAN

Robert A F Thurman is the Jey Tsong Khapa Professor of Indo-Tibetan Buddhist Studies in the Department of Religion at Columbia University, president of the Tibet House US, and president of the American Institute of Buddhist Studies.

He also translates important Tibetan and Sanskrit philosophical writings and lectures and writes on Buddhism, Asian history, and on critical philosophy with a focus on the dialogue between the material and inner sciences of the world's religious traditions.

Time Magazine chose Professor Thurman as one of its 25 most influential Americans in 1997, describing him as a "larger-than-life scholar-activist" and the *New York Times* recently said Thurman "is considered the leading American expert on Tibetan Buddhism." But it's Thurman's unique take on the relevance of Buddhism to American culture and politics, and his wit and creativity in weaving ancient Buddhist wisdom and popular Western ideals, that make his knowledge entertaining and useful as well as informative.

Popularizing the Buddha's teachings is just one of Thurman's creative talents. He is a riveting speaker and an author of many books on Tibet, Buddhism, art, politics, and culture. He is credited with being at the forefront of making Tibetan art accessible and understandable in the West.

Thurman's work and insights are grounded in more than 35 years of serious academic scholarship. He has B.A., A.M. and Ph.D. degrees from Harvard and has studied in Tibetan Buddhist monasteries in India and the US. A long-time advocate of Buddhist monasticism, in 1962, Thurman became the first American ordained as a Tibetan Buddhist monk. He gave up his robes after several years, however, when he discovered he could be most effective in the American equivalent of the monastery, the university.

Thurman's knowledge of Tibetan history and culture is often sought by policy makers. He has testified before the Senate Foreign Relations Committee. Additionally, a plan he authored, which appeared in the *Wall Street Journal* in 1998 as an op-ed piece entitled "Freeing Tibet Is In China's Interest" is regarded by many as a practical, plausible blueprint for peacefully ending the human rights violations and cultural destruction in Tibet.

I first met Robert Thurman in 1985, when he was acting as a translator for the late Tara Tulku Rinpoche at a course offered at the Omega Institute in Rhinebeck, New York. My wife and I felt a philosophical and personal closeness to both him and his wife Nina in their interest in presenting the teachings of the Buddha authentically, but in a modern idiom to positively affect daily living.

It was seven years later that I re-connected with Robert, at the lodge of a hotel near Santa Fe, New Mexico, where H.H. The Dalai Lama was spending the night. I was one of the bodyguards for His Holiness and Robert, a close personal friend to His Holiness, was there to visit. When not on duty walking around His Holiness' compound, I spent the late evening hours talking with Robert about this and that. In particular, he wanted to talk to me about his keen interest in healing and Tibetan medicine, a topic I was writing about at the time.

Since then, we have corresponded occasionally, sometimes about medicine and the retreat he was building in upstate New York. Other times it has been about politics. Thus, when I asked him to participate in this book, the only inhibiting factor was time – which we finally worked out.

Again, the interview took place over Skype with me at home and Robert at his office in New York City.

THE INTERVIEW

Robert: When H.H. Dalai Lama and other teachers gave teachings on the Kalachakra, much was discussed about the idea of a dark age. From your study and observation, do you consider this a dark age and what would you see as the signposts one way or the other? If you see this as a dark age, what are the ways in which people can cope and work with this reality?

Tenzin Bob: I don't think the dark age concept of Buddhism comes only from the Kalachakra. The dark age concept comes from Brahmanism, it's the concept of the Kali Yuga. It connects to their legend in the *Mahabharata* about the war between Pandavas and the Kauravas on the plain of Kurukshetra in the *Bhagavad Gita* section. It teaches a dark age where people have less merit and there is violence and that kind of thing. Buddhism picks that up in terms of the Buddha being here in the most difficult time of this eon of a thousand Buddhas. Our particular Buddha, Sakyamuni, volunteers for this harsh time, due to his special courage. The next Buddha, Maitreya, is born in the Brahmin class because it is more peaceful and the Brahmin intellectuals are then more respected. But our Buddha Sakyamuni is born into the Kshatriya or warrior class because people are more violent and there is more of a warrior mentality.

Buddhism thus fits into the Brahmin cosmology of the Kali Yuga, and that perspective is part of the move in Buddha's teaching to help people turn away from do-gooder-ishness in the world, and focus on achieving their own enlightenment and get away from this world of suffering, of samsara. Of course, when the Buddha and the dharma teachings are present things are a little better for a while. But still, even when the Sakyamuni Buddha is teaching, the people he teaches are said to have low expectations for themselves and for life, are generally rough and unruly and so are normally in various states of fear.

The Kalachakra goes against this perspective by saying that it may look bad, but in the long run the Sakyamuni Buddha has so much power in shaping his world, on shaping his buddhaland (and the *Vimalakirti Sutra* makes the same point) that although it looks bad with wars and holocausts and environmental deterioration, there does come a time when a "golden age" occurs and a lot of people attain enlightenment. But the texts stop short of making this "golden age" permanent. This time is called the period of Shambhala, and it last for 1,800 years. After that things again degenerate, there is an extreme nadir, and then there is a new longer wonderful age, some say after 5,000, some say after 5 million years. That is when Maitreya comes and by that time, the planet is in great shape. So it cycles up and down in the time of a thousand Buddhas. And in those times where there is a dip, like the time which we are in now, a time of trough when things are difficult – in such times individuals should turn their energies towards their own interior and seek to develop themselves and attain enlightenment in spite of the difficulties around them.

Robert: Has that 1,800 years, the period of Shambhala, come and gone?

Tenzin Bob: No, no. The Shambhala prediction is that it will occur about 300 or 400 years from now. But that is a rather minor note in the larger Buddhist message because that is sort of esoteric and is only known by a particular group that know about the Kalachakra or are interested in the Kalachakra Tantra. The larger vision is that things go down from Sakyamuni's time to a really bad time when human beings live only ten years, when they have Bosnia-like mutual fighting, or Iraq-type of violent fighting periodically, when there is much bloodletting and people live in holes in the ground like groundhogs, but with horrible weapons. And it reaches to kind of a mania.

Then the Maitreya, the future Buddha, exerts his energy and then things start to build up in a positive way so that by the time Maitreya comes, there is no violence, the priestly or spiritual class is the highest class and people have long lifespans of thousands of years and the earth is very fruitful and wonderful again. Maitreya attains enlightenment in one day; he experiences no hardship or the need for asceticism. And in the world there is no militarism. So it is like a golden age. And then there is a trough and things go down. Then the next Buddha, the sixth Buddha comes, then later the seventh Buddha and it goes on like that for millions of years until the planet and local universe is destroyed in a big crunch, our sun going supernova. But, while that is happening on this planet in the Buddhist sense, there are other worlds with their own phases and cycles, there are Buddha lands here and there – and anybody who dies and takes rebirth during the time of being in the Bardo, they can go into other universes with no problem.

The Kali Yuga cycle of a particular world sector is controlled by the karma of the beings that tend to be in that world sector – is not determinative in a completely mechanistic way of any one individual. An individual, once they get refuge in the Three Jewels (i.e. Buddha, dharma, and sangha in the Buddhist tradition), once they start evolving consciously toward enlightenment, participating in the inner revolution, then they can turn that in a positive way despite what is going on outside.

Robert: Going back to a point that you made in passing, are you saying that the teachings of Sakyamuni, the historical Buddha that we commonly refer to are, in fact, the teachings of a warrior Buddha? That because we are in a time period where there is low-mindedness and a propensity towards warfare, that the Buddha chose to be reborn into the warrior or Kshatriya caste so that he could teach in a manner appropriate to our capacities?

Tenzin Bob: Yes. That's right. Well, that's always the way it is with Buddhas. Their emanation body manifestations are always appropriate to the time and place. They are, therefore, always born into whichever community and class is the most powerful and the most respected in the world so that when they defect from the preoccupations of that class – in this case, the warrior, kingly class – then no one can say, "Well he was a loser anyway. He has resentment against society. He himself just wasn't the boss." These Buddhas incarnate into the top level and then they leave from that top level, so that their leaving is truly respected and seen as having a real inner meaning.

The *Vimalakirti Sutra*, in an exoteric way, addresses this most clearly and distinctly by the device of the fact that it gives the Buddha's teaching, and then at one point in the sutra some bodhisattvas come to this world from an incense world, which is like a paradise world. When they get here, they think, "Oh, this world really stinks and everybody is suffering and it is horrible and there are no incense trees and there is no samadhi incense. This Buddha must be a real turkey." So they look down on the Buddha. But, Vimalakirti argues that this world, because it is a world of great difficulties, and beings are close to other beings who are suffering, the opportunity to develop compassion is much more available here than in a world where you just sit in samadhi all of the time – your wisdom may be great, but you are so remote from the suffering of others, that your compassion is just a thought. You are not dealing with immediate problems. So there is what

I call a "buddhodicy" (paralleling the notion of "theodicy," a rationalization of suffering in a world created by an omnipotent and good God). This buddhodicy is the Buddha's explanation of suffering within the Mahayana world where buddhas are really powerful, almost divine. Never is it said that buddhas create the world; they are not divine in that sense, but they are divine in their power to shape a world for the benefit of the disciples.

Robert: With respect to the Buddha being from that class, and people of the time of the Sakyamuni Buddha having a warring state of mind, if you were to look at this particular time period and the various wars on the planet, where do you see the rise of fundamentalism or corporate greed fit into the equation?

Tenzin Bob: What I would say is that the people of this world have reached a point where they realize that war is completely self-destructive. It is, in fact, obsolete. Therefore, the Gandhian kind of idea that non-violence is the only viable method for resolving conflict has become widely popular in our world, I would say, except for a group of people who are still leading in a militaristic, rather desperate way. Violence on our planet seems to be dominant because of these people's power and their prejudice that there is no solution to conflict and therefore they are happy to carry on with an obsolete pattern of militarism and so on. They are so completely incompetent; they never win any war, they destroy wherever they go, and it ends up destroying them – which is just part of the laborious process of waking up to the fact that war is obsolete; that violence is obsolete on this planet.

That is where the Buddhist mindset comes in, in the sense of its deepest encouragement of people to understand their reality. Science, even materialistic science, is an exploration of reality which is what the basic Buddhist drive is – to understand reality – because you achieve liberation from suffering when you fully understand reality. So science, even though it thinks of itself as anti-religious or anti-Buddhist, is also exploring reality. And, therefore, researchers in quantum physics have discovered what Buddha knew and taught about so long ago, the uncontrollability of matter and the fact that the subtle energies of the universe can't even be said to be gross matter – we don't even know what they are. Such honest scientists are just at the brink of rediscovering the power of mind. But the people with the power are still in the clutches of these militaristic institutions, industries, and governments. They are beating themselves over the head by flogging the dead horse of trying to conquer each other. They are sort of making money, but they are ruining the quality of their lives in the process; they are paranoid and not enjoying their money at all.

So it is just a matter of time before people do assert their will.

Like right now, the wars that are happening are happening against the will of the majority of all the people in all of the countries involved. The Israeli people don't want war, the Arab people don't want war, the American people don't want war, the European people don't want war, the Russian people don't want war, the Chinese people don't want war. But the little, dominant, autocratic, oligarchic governments and corporations who are addicted to making money out of war, maintaining their power by making people afraid and pretending to protect them, they are having their wars anyway. They are pushing it on the people. They are able to do so by various instruments of control – for the moment. But, basically, they are doing it really badly because they are desperate.

In a way – subconsciously – they know that the kind of power that they have is not true power, which comes from people's assent and people's hearts. People do not assent to what is happening. They do not. There was a great cover of the most recent issue of *Nation* magazine (Jan–Feb 2007) which said, the American people don't want the war, the soldiers don't want the war, the Iraqi people don't want the war, the Iraqi government doesn't want the war, Congress doesn't want the war, the military doesn't really want the war and they keep on firing generals. There are only a few people who want these wars and yet the mass of the people cannot stop them. So, in what meaningful sense is this still a democracy?

The way to stop this, therefore, is to recall or impeach the President and the Vice President, and throw out their cabinet and their asinine various henchmen and women. Nancy Pelosi would then be the president and then we could start to take care of the real business of life. That would also reinstate some level of sanity in the American people and the protection of the rest of the world, and they would realize that we repudiate such leadership and that we did not want these leaders and we did not vote for them. This would be a fresh start for everybody. Right now it seems that we still are unable to do this. But, eventually, that kind of thing will happen.

Robert: The American Congress has passed non-binding resolutions stating that what the President is suggesting, with respect to resolving the Iraqi conflict, is not in the interest of the nation. Does this not make what the President and his administration are doing treasonous?

Tenzin Bob: Yes, treasonous. Of course they are treasonous. They are flagrant liars, they have committed high crimes. They should be impeached. There is absolutely no doubt of this in the eyes of any sane person. But the collective insanity, stimulated by corporate media, militaristic industries, and these nasty leaders, is still gripping people in a state of fear and paralysis where they are unable to do anything. But we'll see. Articles of impeachment have already been introduced by Congressman Kucinich. But they are considered to be oddball, so they don't get much media play. There have also been full-page ads in the *New York Times* and so forth presenting articles of impeachment. But many of these have been impractical. So it will start off with investigations. They will investigate Cheney and get rid of Cheney first – and then Bush. We'll see if it will work. Of course they will definitely be gone by 2008, but by then there will have been worse disasters. Too many more people will be killed and maimed and destroyed by then, so it is really important to get rid of them sooner. But we'll see. We have to hope for the best. We shouldn't be in despair that nobody will see the light or do the right thing. It is important for us to imagine that it could be done. That is very important.

Robert: I am surprised that no one in Congress talks about the Iraqi debacle other than in military terms. Of course, many are calling it a military disaster, a flawed policy. But, if you look at it from the standpoint of corporate profit, it has been immensely profitable, at least in the short term.

Tenzin Bob: I don't think so, except for a very few, in the very short term. In the medium term, it is a complete disaster for the American nation, for the American economy. For various international corporations, multinational corporations who have no loyalty to America... Most of these corporations are not really American, they have their headquarters in places like the Netherland Antilles. They are beyond loyalty to nations and they are ripping off and destroying America. This war is an unmitigated economic disaster for America and the American economy has been artificially propped up for the time being, but is about to go belly up completely. If you have a few euros in your bank account, you are smart. If you have dollars, you are not smart. We are looking at *Brazil* [the movie] here. So, I don't think there has been any general short-term benefit at all.

The people running this war machine are utterly incompetent, except you could say that they have been successful as bank robbers. Thieves, robbers. These corporations are robber companies, piratical institutions. They are like international corsairs. The criminal element is successful on a planet where there is no international law or agency more powerful than them that can operate across international borders. In that sense, they have been getting away with it. But, for America, this war has not been profitable, no way.

Robert: Knowing that the majority of people do not go along with these organizations or corporations, that bespeaks the Buddha nature and common sense of the average person; they can see things for what they are.

Tenzin Bob: [emphatically] YES!

Robert: I must admit that I like the idea of these people being impeached and seeing Nancy Pelosi become the president. We are looking at how these corporate and government powers operate and seem to play off the rising fundamentalisms of the East and the West – which, by the way, I do not see as being all that different – where "manifest destiny" is the same as "jihad"...

Tenzin Bob: That's right...

Robert: Do you see these forces coming into check somehow in the next 50 years or so?

Tenzin Bob: I certainly do, because I think when people come to the brink of self-destruction, they do pull back. If you look back 50 years since the invention and deployment of the first atomic bombs, people who are realistic about the habits of warmongers on our planet can only consider it a supernatural event involving divine intervention that there has been no nuclear war for over 60 years. It has been a completely astounding thing. And that proves that people are not just driven to react in the same way and they can actually restrain themselves; they develop the mind to try something different. I think on every level that will increase as the situation gets more and more dire, and within this decade I think there will be a major shift, or even sooner.

But this is pure speculation. I don't claim to be a prophet. One thing is that it is the duty of people not to allow themselves – under the guise of pretending that they are being realistic – to concede to the desperation that has everyone in its grip and the feeling that everything is hopeless. That single mental function as it resonates out to the minds of others, that thought that it is all hopeless, we really have a duty not to indulge in it, not to just keep coming up with the same old, "Oh, it's all impossible," and "I'm realistic and it's never going to be good." We have an emotional tendency like that because that is how we are brainwashed by the elite that dominates us with fear. But, as Franklin Roosevelt said years ago, the only thing to fear is fear itself, because that is what makes us susceptible, leads to paranoia – and then it becomes a self-fulfilling prophecy.

So we have to have the insight that nowadays it is more realistic to be idealistic. It is unrealistic to pretend to succumb to realpolitik, a fake hard-nosed realism. To expect the worst is what is really unrealistic and self-destructive, since it makes us work to create the worst, on the excuse that it is inevitable. We have the duty not to go there. People's deep realism is necessary in order to save everybody, because the reality is that the war thing is self-destructive. Nobody wins it. People did once fight wars to win them. But, nobody is going to win any more and nobody is winning any of them, and that will continue to be the case.

Robert: Because you travel extensively and meet people who could be defined as agents of change in the world, what trends do you see people involved with that can make a difference in creating or supporting the change you are describing?

Tenzin Bob: I see people trying to control their own minds and people trying to achieve real happiness for themselves and for others; beginning to rediscover their connectedness to each other and to nature and to get away from these ideologies that teach and confirm people in their delusion of somehow being essentially separate from the world and from each other. Those ideologies are the really destructive ones. And I see that becoming much, much better. In fact I see the dharma, without it being called Buddhism, as reality, and a more realistic way of being, a realistic awareness of body, speech, and mind as becoming more widely prevalent in the world, as the dire consequences of the unrealistic way of living of body, speech, and mind become more and more evident. That is what I see.

Robert: Going outside the social and political sphere to look at the environment, although Al Gore's film, *An Inconvenient Truth*, along with results of the latest research point to the human contribution to the problem of global warming, regardless of the origin, how do you see global warming having an impact on the social and political realities that you speak of?

Tenzin Bob: It's part of it. Global warming is the greed side as war is the hate side. Corporate greed and source depletion, overpopulation, that is on the greed side and the hate side is the war side. That's all a part of waking people up; in a way, showing them their impact. Al Gore, you know, our president-in-exile, wrote that book in the 1980s, *Earth in the Balance*, that really is the guide to the issue which is why he should be president. He should run again now. He should really be the president of this country. Maybe he needs to be the head of the UN or something or some new agency. I don't know. But he needs to continue his work of waking people up to the consequences of their actions; the historical failure of human beings achieving power through the expansion of their cleverness with technology without enough wisdom. They have now come to a point where they can destabilize their entire environment and destroy themselves. People have to wake up to that and realize their connectedness, turn away and work in the opposite direction. When they do wake up, I think that the danger of the situation will call them to do that.

Another problem at this point is that our former colonial protégés, the Chinese, the Indians, the Vietnamese, and others who Westerners had empires over, they are still caught up in trying to imitate our century-old empires, and it is hard to try to stop them from imitating us and making the same errors. They are so huge in population and energy that if they pollute the way we polluted and utilize and destroy resources the way we did, then we are all really done for. The coal being madly burned in China now is a really destructive thing. So maybe it's better that Gore is not president and should try to create some kind of forum where he can speak to non-Americans as well as to Americans. Maybe that is the next step for him. I hope so.

But I am very positive. I think we'll all manage. We're going to awaken. And anyway it is our duty to be positive – because the greatest danger is despair. The reason people are not doing anything about these things is that they are misunderstanding Al Gore – they think that he is implying that there is nothing you can do about any of these things. There is no way you could do anything about it. Once you do that, then you think, well, I might as well light my fire, burn my coal, or do whatever and enjoy myself in the short run, because in the long run we are all doomed anyway. That is the great danger: cynicism based on despair.

I am not a prophet, you know. These are mostly prophetic questions that you are asking. I know you are asking for opinions and they may be quite appropriate. But these are not necessarily the dharma perspective. The dharma perspective is, you know, everybody can go ahead and kill themselves and they will just be reborn and they will have to deal with this on the next planet. They can destroy this entire planet and then they will be reborn and suffer again on the next planet. So they might as well wake up and try to deal with it on this planet. That would be more intelligent. And I think they will do that – with the help of the angels and the *dakinis*.

Robert: I know your answers can only be opinions, Tenzin, but because of your dharma knowledge and practice, they come with a foundation that I think gives them a unique level of credibility and value in heeding.

Another issue that comes up and is discussed is the matter of the rise in power of China in the 21st century. What are your thoughts on this?

Tenzin Bob: That is a complete myth. There is no rise of China. China is merely a slave depot for Western corporate greed in the last phases of colonialism. The last residence of colonialism and Western imperialism is converting certain leaders, buying off certain corrupt leaders of these countries with the offer of sharing some of the imperialist wealth so that they will suppress the people of those countries and enslave them. The ploy of using cheap labor in export platforms in China has been used to destroy the middle class and the labor movements in America. These corporate colonialists are only mad that they have been unable to break Europe's labor movement and middle class – yet they still hope to.

So, for those previously colonialized countries, after we invaded them and exploited them for centuries, the last thing we are doing is to let them think that they are "developing" by being industrial in a self-destructive way. But, there is only a group of maybe a 100 to 150 million people in each of China and India that have been brought up to the material level of some sort of Westerner. To get that money, they have served as representatives of the imperial corporation power and have destroyed their own people's health, their gardens and fields, their water and air – using up their resources and enslaving their people. In the case of China, supposedly "rising," there are over 1.2 billion people who are being wasted; they don't have clean air to breathe, clean water to drink, their earth is polluted, and their land is being taken away for high-rise petroleum-based buildings and factories – it is a complete disaster. China is being destroyed. This last wave of destruction is occurring. You cannot breathe in an Asian city nowadays with the uncontrolled emissions in the air; 50 percent of the population with lung diseases; people's home places are being destroyed. And yes, there seem to be some Chinese individuals getting the wealth, former

Communist Party members, and they are ready to go to Switzerland before times get too bad with their people.

So this rise-of-China idea is a myth. It is a perpetuation of the myth that the industrial, imperial lifestyle raises the standard of the living of the slaves. That has always been a myth. The slaves have never really enjoyed this. And on top of it all, the supposed owners of the slaves themselves are enslaved by the system, and live in mental distress they go to lengths to deny.

From the brave Harry Wu's work, just look at the figures – 127 million – a conservative estimate, of the Lao Gai labor camp system in China, and there are about 250 million people working in non-union, slave-exploited, five-cents-a-day factories, often seven days a week, working in dangerous conditions without any gas masks with pollution and plastics dust and chemicals and what have you. Then there are 300–400 million unemployed running loose. And 500–600 million desperate peasants who don't have water in their rivers and the smog is flowing in every direction and people selling their blood, drawing it with dirty needles and spreading AIDS, and SARS and animal flu and I don't know what. And people call that a rise?

Robert: So when you listen to NPR (National Public Radio) and the 10 percent increase in the Chinese economy…

Tenzin Bob: Economics is an insane science. Economists are deeply insane. Economics doesn't calculate the cost to the environment of the pollution, nor of the depletion of the resources. It simply considers the environment an endless cash account to draw upon. Ecology and economics do not connect. I do not know if you know that. Economics does not pay any attention to the impact of their economics and their so-called "product" and the waste of the product. I mean it is really absurd, the thinking of these people, I don't care if they get Nobel prizes, they are cheerleaders of the destruction of all life.

Robert: I guess it's like looking at the stock market and it's so-called boom, and realizing that it is only booming for people invested in the arms trade.

Tenzin Bob: Exactly.

Robert: One of the last issues I would like to bring up with you has to do with the ethical debacle in science and medicine around the issue of stem cell research. From a strictly philosophical point of view, how does Buddhism define and look at stem cell research?

Tenzin Bob: Stem cell research is perfectly fine, from the Buddhist perspective. If people can find some medicine out of stem cells – if they can restrain themselves from going at it in such a way that they run around and buy people's organs or tap the spinal fluid of prisoners in some prison or concentration camp – if they don't use it in some atrocious manner, then it's all fine. That could be very good. There is not a problem. The Dalai Lama was asked what he thought about cloning. He said, "Why would people want to make more people? They don't take care of the ones that are made naturally in wombs. So, why should we make more of them?" It's not that there is some intrinsic moral problem with it. It's like, why would you make more people when you can't take care of the ones that you breed normally? In terms of stem cell research, as long as it is not a highly rarified thing for just a tiny elite, it could help people.

The Buddhist faith is that the more you understand reality, the more liberated from suffering you are, and if you study cells, genes, atoms, and subatomic energies, the better – the more the better. People will refuse knowledge, of course, and they will misuse it, whether they have good knowledge or bad knowledge. But the more knowledge they have, the better chance there is of people thriving and doing well.

So, this is really a red-herring type of issue – are we letting sick people die to save some nonviable embryos? It's some cuckoo thing of people who are not wanting to think for themselves, that's all. Just a know-nothing George Bush stopping stem cell research in order to seem pious. Meanwhile he has contributed to the death of probably a million Iraqis and maiming and killing at least 50,000–60,000 Americans – not just the supposed 2,000–3,000. That is just propaganda statistics. When you maim someone for life and they have to live in a basket forever, that's just like killing them. The most conservative study, coming out of a Johns Hopkins study some time ago mentioned 650,000 Iraqis, but then there are the many killed by the sanctions since the first Bush war. This is criminal behavior. This is a war crime we are talking about here. That is really too bad. And everybody knows it is, except for a few deluded people who can only react with denial and paranoia, and they can't face the enormity of their crimes. Somehow we have to undo this, heal and solve it. It's going to be a big job, but we are capable of it. We can do it.

Robert: Looking at your vision, Tenzin, I am reminded of our most recent trip to Europe, where we observed a real fusion, a cross-fertilization of cultures taking place – being in France and seeing high French fashion accented with Afghan beads and colors, French restaurants besides kebab houses, fusion music, TV networks presenting real international news rather than just hearing what is on FOX or the major networks. We even got to watch Al Jazeera – the supposed network of choice for terrorists as this administration would have you believe.

So there is this real coming together, and I don't mean some kind of homogenization. At the same time, listening to the news, there is a fear of encroaching fundamentalism in Europe. How do you see this fusion continuing? How do you see that it will work?

Tenzin Bob: We're getting there. We'll get there. Don't give up. We'll all get there. There is no way out of it.

The Europeans are ahead because they had a truly terrible war on their territory and they saw obliteration happening all around them. The Russians also did. They had the Nazis all the way to Stalingrad. That has only been some kind of remote reality for us here. We blithely talk about being a superpower and so on, but we haven't really won any war since World War II, and that only with the help of millions of Russians and Chinese, among many others. And as for this current situation in Iraq, we have already lost, catastrophically. We have businesses that are making money out of it and propaganda media that tries to glorify it. But, we'll learn. And, we'll get there. We'll catch up to them. Let us hope that we can learn with all the information at our fingertips, become more realistic without having to experience everything exploding all around us. Learn, and stand up and change things joyfully and peacefully ahead of time!

Robert: This has been very positive. I want to thank you very much.

Going Down
the Mountain

According to the Buddha, we are basically good and we all possess the capacity for enlightenment. We want to be happy, and we soon discover that in making those around us happy, we are even happier. And we also seek to understand – to know who we are and why we are the way we are.

But, not fully grasping our interconnectedness with all of life that surrounds us, we can get some funny, distorted, sometimes perverse, even dangerous ideas about our importance in the scheme of things. We take ourselves far too seriously and build up a world-view with us in the center. To support this world-view we employ a selected knowledge base of fact and faith, backed by force (arising from our will, wealth, charisma, status, weaponry, or a combination thereof) legitimated by our very own facts and faith. There are tangible and mysterious reasons to justify our position. And, from this position, we think that our friends are those who help to fortify the walls around us, that our enemies are those who have the potential to take those walls down, and then there are those who just pass by. We don't notice them and they don't notice us. Even if they do notice us, what does it matter? They are of little consequence one way or the other.

So it goes – in families, neighborhoods, and nations. Without clear understanding, living in a distorted reality, we cannot help but create and perpetuate sickness, poverty, and warfare. If we were to succumb to a lesser view of human heart and potential, we might conclude that that is all that we can expect. After all, isn't so much of history a documentation of pestilence, wars, and tragedies? How many times has history repeated itself? And yet there have been great and powerful teachers, books and words of wisdom, extraordinary music, profound breakthroughs in science. Superstitions of one generation have often been dissolved in discoveries in our physical world, but also within our inner world. And so there have been heretics of faith and science. Fact and faith have changed and changed again. In each generation there are some that want to do good with such, and those who, still seeing themselves as the centers of their universe, chose more selfish, myopic goals. This is nothing new. But in this time, our present time, there is something more that is added to the well-trodden plot of the human drama.

The fact is that in our quest for happiness, our quest to know, we have created a world that is shrinking. Inter-connection and interconnectedness is undeniable. The constant of change in a world where new knowledge is gained and old knowledge lost, in a matter of a generation, shows the fleeting, impermanent nature of our very existence – or at least the way of being we have been clutching to with both hands. Advances in the speed and ease of travel, advances in the speed and ease of communication and the sharing of information, mean that we really (or virtually) do bump into more and more people, cultures, and nations. And each holds themselves as the center of their respective universes.

Thus, we have created for ourselves a rather interesting quandary. In contrast to the absolute, universal truths that most civilized cultures have agreed upon since the dawn of time, the standards that cultures and societies now hold up or hold onto, as a measure of importance or way of being, have become relativized, challenged by rubbing shoulders with other forms of civilized society, living to the tunes of other drummers. The intensity of our time is such that there are some who desperately are holding onto world-views that are crashing down around them. Facts and faith are being expanded upon, turned inside out, vaporized, or hybridized. We are in an amazingly fecund age of cross-pollinatation – a mongrelization destined to forever blur the lines of race, place, and ethnicity. Caught in the speed of our own transformation – and as if to demonstrate our own shock, awkwardness, and struggle with this loss or annihilation of personal and cultural identity – is our simultaneous creation of weapons of mass destruction. Such weapons are a metaphor of our inner turmoil – our innocent belief in a past, which, if we were to look at it more closely and honestly, we would see as having never been static or ideal, versus the denial of this truth, this mark of impermanence.

Although many of the world's spiritual traditions speak of golden ages, the cyclic nature of time, and the possibility that we could return to such a time, right now, we are not there. Furthermore, exclusivity – a shrinking away from and embracing a more fundamentalist approach to fact and faith, in an age of weapons of mass destruction and environmental collapse in the face of our demands for overconsumption – is not a viable option. Too much is at stake. The have-nots can no longer just stand by or bend over for the want-it-alls. For life to return to balance, to step back from the precipice and be able to come to terms with (and possibly shift) the intensity of the impending global crises that each of these teachers says we shall be looking at in the coming years, we need to take ourselves in hand. We need to be inclusive, not just of the other humans around us, but all of life. The ethic of inclusivity that supports greater cooperation amongst people, cultures, nations, is the same inclusivity that must be adopted in returning to a way of being that recognizes our dependency on our very planet and all of its species, flora, and fauna for survival.

After "Going Up the Mountain," I returned with the words of the teachers you have just read. But, more importantly for me, personally, is that not only did I feel enriched and inspired by their words, but I have also been emboldened to speak more clearly my thoughts and feelings on these various issues as well. Thus, what follows is both a summation of what I believe the salient points are from these teachers, and my own musings, which I hope contribute to what these masters have so graciously offered.

ON A "DARK AGE" AND WHAT TO DO ABOUT IT...

Regardless of whether one calls this time a "dark age" or a "degenerate age," we are clearly facing challenges. Theravadin tradition seems to point to the idea that we are in a golden period at the beginning of a dark age which will become more evident by the middle of this century. This coincides with H.H. Kunzig Shamar Rinpoche's warning that if education continues to degrade and common sense is lost, our leaders will be powerless or inept in being able to stop those of more insidious intentions with barbaric inclinations. Contributing to, or signs of, this being a possible if not probable future is the degradation of education, unbridled, unabashed and well-marketed me-ism and materialism, a fracturing of the family structure and bonds of affection, and the rise of simplistic faiths in the form of Eastern and Western fundamentalisms.

Classic texts mention a diminishing of life expectancy in degenerate times. Of course, we notice that infant mortality is down in general and we have more and more medical interventions for illnesses of age that used to kill. But we are seeing the development of old-age and chronic degenerative illnesses in young people: heart disease, diabetes, obesity, and cancers. Robert Thurman mentions how the texts tell of a time when people live to be only ten years of age. Most of us may not see how this could even be believable. But there are any number of signs that we are getting closer and closer to this reality.

Consider the fact that we are seeing children at an earlier age develop secondary sexual characteristics and that the youngest birth that we currently have on record is by a nine-year-old. At the same time, college campus clinics are reporting more and more young men who complain of impotence. The sperm count of these young men is diminishing. There is also a growing number of women reporting extreme dysmenorrhea and more and more couples wanting to have children find that they are incapable of doing so without some kind of fertility boosting. Besides the reproductive anomalies in our own species, scientists are finding more examples of bisexual abnormalities in amphibious and aquatic life. Finally, if we wish to disregard all of these other signs, we can just turn our attention to Africa where orphaned ten-year-olds who are HIV positive become the parents to their infant siblings, or become sex workers, or start families of their own at puberty, and die soon after.

Another sign of a degenerate age is where the stability and richness of natural resources is threatened and diminishing. Whilst many in the environmental movement have for years been voicing their concerns about CO_2 emissions, oil consumption, air and water pollution, agribusiness, and the gradual swallowing up of available farmland, recent scientific and political discussions on the reality and implications of global warming have brought these and other environmental matters front and center to industry and world governments. Coupled with the diminishing environmental resources are desperation and insecurity which undermine our sense of well-being and place and spawn territorial conflicts over resources.

Of course, several of the teachers pointed out that life has always been precarious and that the causes and conditions for such suffering are nothing new. The Tibetan Rinpoches are well aware of this fact, but step back and look at the situation from a more cosmic perspective. For them, it is more a matter of degree. Yes, suffering and all the causes of suffering have been with us since forever. But, when suffering accumulates to the point of inducing global crisis, whilst we may celebrate and be appreciative of the fantastic opportunities to study, grow, and transform our lives, part of that transformation involves a willingness to dive into the fray and get one's hands dirty, wet, or bloody in making efforts to help those around us whose hearts, minds, and bodies are in desperate need of healing. And, if we choose not to engage in efforts to turn things around, we may be yet another civilization that disappears from the face of the earth. Then again, considering where we are, this might happen anyway.

Although it would be nice to imagine that when wisdom is generously offered we would learn, most of the time we ignore such pearls until we experience enough discomfort to provoke us to pay closer attention. The best teacher is, therefore, disaster. And as many of the teachers speak in terms of us being perched on the edge of disaster, it would seem that there needs to be a two-pronged approach to working through, and making more manageable, the times that we face for as many people as possible. One approach has to do with mustering the courage, will, and ethical resolve to act. Here we are talking about developing a more comprehensive and cooperative coming together of political and economic forces, to form a sane consensus on how to most benefit the world and its inhabitants in general. The second prong is education – a more long-term goal, but necessary as a key in developing our ability and resolve to divert or minimize such times.

I am in agreement with Robert Thurman when he says that not only have we outgrown the leaders of small minds and confused hearts to continue as the wielders of power on this planet, we cannot survive in a sustainable way if we follow their example or lead. Thurman contends that such individuals are on their way out – maybe not as soon as many of us would like, but the trend is there. I think this trend is due to there being a number of powerful and influential people in the world with resources and economic savvy, an ever-watchful global media that more easily exposes scams, corruption, despotism, and the like, and a grass-roots movement in many countries that has demonstrated, both in the East and West, that they have the political capital and network to be agents of change. Whilst state- and corporate-run media give little if any coverage to protests and gatherings with political, economic, and ecological concerns, the numbers of people involved in such gatherings has swelled far beyond the numbers that were seen during the protests of the 1960s, and their presence has been picked up by independent media outlets and the information superhighway – the Internet. Thus it comes as no surprise that concerned repressive regimes are trying to limit, censure, or raise the charge of Internet access. To become a part of the organizations and movements that seek change, that see obvious causes or contributors to sickness, poverty, and warfare, is a noble gesture whose fruits are too often undersung, but are making a difference.

The small-minded and confused-hearted people who make up the elites that such groups are trying to influence are not – for the most part – stupid. They are often well educated and have all of the facts and figures that progressives use as their ammunition against them. But it is an historical fact that breakthroughs in science, medicine, technology and other forms of understanding have often been initially greeted with resistance, if not overt oppression. Oftentimes the reasons given for such oppression have been religious or said to be for the common good. More often than not, the real issues have been power and economics. Consider Galileo. Consider the electric car.

All this said, I cannot be overly optimistic that small-minded ambitious people, and the organizations they create, will be wholly eliminated from the halls of power and influence. And there will be those who will blindly and naively abdicate their responsibility through ignorance, fear, or other confused emotions. Generally speaking, until we sufficiently, both individually and collectively, develop our own inner resources, we shall continue to inappropriately rely on sources outside ourselves. In the long run, such dependency is a problem and leads to personal fanaticism, groveling, and a whole host of organiza-tional and societal problems: backbiting, intrigue, power trips and games, infighting – the problems of self-importance and organizational inbreeding.

Any system, if it truly touts democracy and freedom of thought, should have inbuilt mechanisms to deconstruct itself when followers or citizens are ready to take on more authority in their own lives. In the context of governmental models and blueprints, the American Constitution, which owes many of its most far-reaching egalitarian principles to the Iroquois people of North America, stands as an example of a document that sets up guidelines and measures to protect citizens from government officials run amok. In America today, it is sad to see men and women of such low caliber and morals strive to eviscerate this document. It remains to be seen if they can succeed.

In the meantime, people with good intentions fueled by these ideals must continue their working efforts to ensure the best possible future they can imagine – if not for themselves, then, in keeping with Native American principles, for generations who have not yet come. As part of their efforts and as a sign of their maturity and growth, they must develop the sensibility to remain ever vigilant in watching out for, exposing, and turning back those whose minds are small and hearts confused. This may not stop the ascent of such people at times, for unless we are enlightened, we are all of somewhat small mind and confused heart, and there are times when there are traits of ours that are called upon and needed regardless of how neurotic or self-centered we are. For times change and the needs we have in situations can change individually and collectively. In matters amongst human communities with ever-changing needs and aspirations, there are times when we need peacemakers and times that we need warriors. However, very little is accomplished of worth if our peacemakers turn out to be cowards and our warriors, thugs. So, we need to pay attention. We must heed the adage, "Power corrupts and absolute power corrupts absolutely." We need to stay engaged and when we find that those in whom we place our trust are not deserving of it, we must have the ability and will to stop them in their tracks sooner rather than later. Perhaps then we can avert some of the harshness and hard times that are inherited and often need to be undone or atoned for by future generations.

To augment and support the efforts of those who look to a brighter day for all, there must also be efforts to make available more and better education. This is the second prong.

The style of education we are speaking of is not the education of memorization and zeros and ones. That is the education of automatons and future drones. An overemphasis on technological competence, "teaching to the test," and – in America – funding cuts to bolster military spending have undermined and undervalued a holistic learning process. I fear that the lowering of educational standards, seen particularly in the US, will further what H.H. Kunzig Shamar Rinpoche sees as the tendency for Western education to create "machine" minds that leave individuals mentally impoverished, easily swayed from without, and thus seduced by simplistic faiths or promises of greater fulfillment with excitement through consumption.

In this scenario, fundamentalism and addiction are inevitable. Simplistic answers to life's dilemmas easily spawn cultures where manifest destiny and jihad are the external manifestation of inner confusion, poverty, and turmoil. Children educated in this way will be far less self-reliant and in awe of superheroes and saviors; the perfect opportunity for the rise of future Hitlers, Stalins, Bushes, and the like.

We need to encourage education to understand the inner workings of the mind – philosophy, arts, music, physical education, and meditative skills. The ideal graduate of such education is intelligent, robust, reasonably sensitive, emotionally mature, resourceful, and productive. Such education, now more available to larger and larger numbers of people because of the explosion of information technologies, has historically never been the mainstay of what has been available to the average person. It has usually been reserved for society's elite or for those they select and label as gifted. Democratic, socialist, and communist system-based governments have tried to level the playing field in one way or the other. In the US, scholarships, grants, social service assistance and programs, and affirmative action have been some of the means by which there have been attempts to level the playing field. A public version of what I would call holistic learning has been available in one form or another with the inclusion – wherever possible – of arts, music, physical education, social studies, home economics, and health along with the sacred cows of education – math and science.

In progressive schools throughout the world, there have been remarkable discoveries in the areas of brain function and learning that corroborate what the ancients knew about the learning process. Thus, private schools offering early education models, such as Montessori and Waldorf, are creating children who are bright, inquisitive and well adapted to absorb the sheer volume of information it takes to navigate the modern world. And there are still schools of higher education where the humanities hold a hallowed place in the curriculum. We do see young, bright minds wanting to stay engaged in the world; kids who are concerned for the planet they live on and the future. In many ways, I am intrigued by the vast array of non-governmental organizations (NGOs), charities and citizen watch-dog organizations that have mushroomed over the last 40 years. More thought and organization is going into how to tend to the poor, the ill, and the disfranchised.

However, if our systems of education remain lacking or insufficiently funded to benefit the greatest number of our children, the democratic ideal will continue to elude us as a reality. Representative democracy, where an elected elite speaks for the interests of the many is the next best thing. But that, again, depends on a relatively well-informed voting electorate and elected officials of intelligence with moral and ethical standards who act altruistically and on behalf of those who have placed them into positions of prominence and power. If the voting electorate are not well educated, if they are bombarded and swayed by the voluminous bilge of well-funded sound bites and ad campaigns, and if elected officials are not much better educated themselves or are not of the moral fiber and caliber to act beyond self-interest, then honestly, what chance does democracy really have?

To have confidence in, and call upon, the enlightened potential that each being possesses, those who are more progressive, those who participate in grass-roots efforts around the globe must make strong endeavors to educate, draw attention to and hopefully evoke participation and responsiveness in those who are innocently unaware, self-preoccupied, numbed, sedated, or indifferent to their world. This must be done at all levels; in our homes, our communities, our halls of power, our own nations, and wherever we feel we may have some influence.

In most countries in the world, there is little confidence in politicians or governments. Most people have a commonsense view that their media is controlled by interests who are primarily out for themselves. Thus, what I have described here is what some see as the norm, if not inevitable. But, as many of the writers in this book have said, giving in to this situation as reality is to already surrender – to turn the world over to those who seem not to fully comprehend the magnitude of their contribution to human suffering. We cannot do this. We need to turn to ideals, to dreams, affirmations, and visualizations of something better. In a sense, such ideals are still alive in the psyche of Americans. For Americans are probably the last hold-outs in believing that a responsive, democratically elected government is possible, and that politicians should actually be true servants to the will and needs of the many. We get shocked and hurt when we find out that our leaders and our government are not living up to our dreams. This makes us seem foolish in the eyes of many around the world.

But are not such dreams noble? Are they not worth pursuing? If we are to mobilize sufficient resources and energy to properly engage the many issues that we face that can well be the undoing of us all, might it not actually be wisdom to fuel our efforts with such dreams?

Conclusion

THE GIFT OF OUR TIME...

The "gift" of this time is that never have we been so fully capable of standing witness to our own folly on such a global level. Never has it been true that greed didn't cause someone harm; that self-centered desire and ambition did not create suffering, both for others as well as oneself, either in the short or long run. If we are to believe the eastern teachings of karma, then it may just be that the number of people experiencing new and mutating forms of sickness, poverty, and living with the threat of being engulfed by war zones is the fruition of greed, ambition, and self-centeredness since – as Buddhists would say – beginningless time.

Even if this is just a philosophical viewpoint that can be dismissed by those who are either smarter or those who do not believe at all in such notions, our mass media is able to put in our faces the results of such actions. We are mercilessly or compassionately – depending on how you want to see it – bombarded with digital images on screens and in papers, blogospheres providing real-time reporting and commentary on what happens to cultures and regions when greed, ambition, and self-centeredness are partially or wholly, overtly or covertly the motivating forces. Diamonds are mined with little concern for the welfare or safety of the miners and their families, oil is extracted and its consumption unchecked, humans are used as guinea pigs for pharma-ceuticals or insufficiently safety-tested food and products, election processes are tampered with, foreign operatives help to topple a government, and so on.

Because we are now capable of the total global annihilation of ourselves, and a number of other species along the way, with our weapon cleverness – and have possibly ratcheted up the forces of nature with our own man-made spin to set in motion environmental events more cataclysmic than they might have been otherwise – it is a time of tremendous opportunity. We are in a time when rapid growth of human heart and spirit is possible if not essential; if not for our own time, for the future that our children will inherit.

Although in reading the various interviews you may have preferred the vision of some teachers more than others, my own bias is to heed particularly the words of the Tibetan Rinpoches. Whilst their English and use of language may have seemed simpler or simplistic at times, their wisdom is very, very deep. Thus, when they look at the coming 50 to 100 years and speak of big changes, of harder times for humanity in general where barbarity and cruelty may – temporarily – get the better of us, I do not look at this as some pessimistic vision, a predetermined nightmare that we must endure. For one thing, when such teachers say these words, they say them with a profound compassion and love for us all. And, by and large, they are tremendously happy. They are not "eternal" optimists, nor do they wear rose-colored spectacles. Rather, they see our goodness, our awakening potential as birthright; a limitless source from which all of us will eventually, in our own way and time, manifest awakening for the benefit of all.

At the same time, whereas I could not accept as readily the more optimistic vision of what is to come espoused by some of the Western teachers from the wellspring of their Buddhist practice, yet a message was conveyed loud and clear – *pessimism is poison*. Change is afoot and if you want to be happy and see the happiness of others, it is time to be fearless and give of ourselves. And there is no time to waste.

Each of us has gifts. Each of us has talents. We must each discover our own wealth and potential. This requires inner exploration and a willingness to use what we have gleaned and mined from this exploration and apply it to the world that we find ourselves in. What our world looks like, how it feels to us, its dictates, are none other than our inner conflicts and confusion playing themselves out in the phantasm before us. For some of us this may feel grand, for others of us this may seem horrible. Regardless, it all changes as we change. And, if we want to see things change for the better, we have to want change and act on that want, which includes committing ourselves to try to eradicate in ourselves the greed, ambition, and self-centeredness that will always ensure the downfall of our fortunes. If we cannot muster the courage to confront these things within ourselves to save ourselves, then perhaps we would do better to think of our children and future generations. For our action or inaction will certainly contribute to their world.

In the immensity of the responsibility we all share in such times, I am reminded of a timely encounter with a dear friend. We ran into each other at a local supermarket. Our friendship had begun in the summer of 2004, when we both became a part of a local presidential campaign for a candidate that both of us were inspired by. Inevitably we found ourselves immersed in a conversation about the war, the US government, the environment, and other such matters that seemed so dire.

His eyes got bigger and bigger as we talked and finally he just blurted out, "I can't talk about this any more. It just overwhelms me and then I get depressed." And so I backed off; we spoke of pleasantries and grandbabies and parted ways.

Feeling incomplete and wanting to make the final taste in his mouth more positive, I caught up with him in the parking lot. And I told him this…

I can't just escape altogether from what I see around me. And yet, if I only focus on the news and all of the challenges we face all of the time, it does get overwhelming. So, there are times when all I feel I can do is continue my spiritual practices, exercise, take care of the immediate needs of my family and tasks at hand, and just appreciate what goodness there is in being alive.

But, then, after a while, I will turn on the news. I take it in and let it break my heart. It reminds me that I can always do more.

And with renewed strength and resolve, I try to do what I can.

Pockets of Light

A RESOURCE GUIDE

There are any number of organizations and agencies around the world where people can learn, volunteer, work for, and make donations to benefit others, the environment, and regions of the planet. For the most part all of them are worthwhile and contribute something positive for a future world – for a brighter tomorrow, no matter how far in the distance that may seem.

To traverse the times that we are in and make effective any of the changes that are needed for the future will require both skill and wisdom. Each of the teachers that has contributed to this book holds a wisdom that makes it possible for each of us to endure, even transform our hearts and minds to see the picture from a larger, more enlightened perspective. Without such wisdom, without the peace and equanimity that they offer, it is not hard to get sucked into a chasm of cynicism, depression, or indifference.

Thus, to honor their contribution here, but mostly to help you, the reader, avail yourself of their teachings and methods, I am pleased to include a listing of their organizations, websites, contact information, as well as a partial listing of their books and publications.

H.H. Kunzig Shamar Rinpoche
Main American Center
449 Galloping Path
Natural Bridge, VA 24578
USA
Telephone: +1 540-464-5117
Fax: +1 540-463-4227
Newsletter: *The Path*
Website: http://www.bodhipath.org

Ven. Tarthang Tulku Rinpoche
Nyingma Institute
1815 Highland Place
Berkeley CA 94709
USA
Telephone: +1 510-843-6812
Email: Nyingma-Institute@nyingma.org
Website: http://www.nyingma.org

Selected books by Tarthang Tulku Rinpoche
Knowledge of Freedom: Time To Change, Dharma Publishing
Skillful Means: Pattens for Success, Dharma Publishing
Gesture of Balance, Bookpeople
Time, Space and Knowledge, Dharma Publishing
Knowledge of Time and Space, Dharma Publishing
Annals of the Nyingma Lineage in America: 1975–1977 (Volume 2),
Dharma Publishing

Geshe Tenzin Wangyal Rinpoche
Ligmincha Institute
313 2nd St. SE, Suite #207
Charlottesville VA 22902
USA
Telephone: +1 434-977-6161
Fax: +1 434-977-7020
Email: Ligmincha@aol.com

Selected books by Tenzin Wangyal Rinpoche
Healing with Form, Energy and Light, Snow Lion Publications
The Tibetan Yogas of Dream and Sleep, Snow Lion Publications
Tibetan Sound Healing, Sounds True Inc.
Wonders of the Natural Mind, Snow Lion Publications

Geshe Michael Roach
Diamond Mountain University
Diamond Mountain
PO Box 37
Bowie AZ 85605
USA
Telephone: +1 520-232-2024
Email: inquiries@diamondmtn.org
Website: http://diamondmtn.org

Selected books by Geshe Michael
The Diamond Cutter, Diamond Cutter Press
The Garden, Doubleday
The Tibetan Book of Yoga, Doubleday

With Christie McNally
How Yoga Works, Diamond Cutter Press
Essential Yoga Sutra, Doubleday

With Sermey Khensur Geshe Lobsang Tharchin
The Principal Teachings of Buddhism, Mahayana Sutra and Tantra Press
Preparing for Tantra, Mahayana Sutra and Tantra Press

Ven. Ajahn Amaro
Abhayagiri Buddhist Monastery
16201 Tomki Road
Redwood Valley CA 95470
USA
Telephone: +1 707-485-1630
Website: http://www.abhayagiri.org
Articles and downloadable books are available on the website.

Selected books by Ajahn Amaro
Rugged Interdependency, Abhayagiri Buddhist Monastery
Who Will Feed the Mice?, Abhayagiri Buddhist Monastery

Roshi Joan Halifax
Upaya Zen Center
1404 Cerro Gordo Road
Santa Fe NM 87501
USA
Telephone: +1 505-986-8518
Fax: +1 505-986-8528
Email: upaya@upaya.org
Website: http://www.upaya.org

For articles, interviews, newsletters, and poetry of Roshi Joan, please visit the website.

Ven. Thubten Chodron
Sravasti Abbey (US)
PO Box 20644
Seattle WA 98102-1644
USA
Telephone: +1 509-447-5549

Sravasti Abbey, c/o Ang Hwee Leng (Asia)
Blk 3, Rivervale Link, #02-17
Singapore 545119
Telephone: +65 6489-5646 or 9798-6389
Websites: http://www.sravastiabbey.org and
http://www.thubtenchodron.org

Selected books by Venerable Thubten Chodron
Taming the Mind, Snow Lion Publications
Buddhism for Beginners, Snow Lion Publications
Open Heart, Clear Mind, Snow Lion Publications
Working with Anger, Snow Lion Publications
Transforming Problems, part of the video series "Discovering Buddhism"
Cultivating a Compassionate Heart: The Yoga Method of Chenrezig, Snow Lion Publications
How To Free Your Mind: Tara The Liberator, Snow Lion Publications

Christopher Titmuss

7 Denys Road

Totnes

Devon

TQ9 5TJ

UK

http://www.christophertitmuss.org

http://www.insightmeditation.org

http://www.dharmafacilitators.org (for dedicated practictioners)

http://www.livingdharma.info (mentor online programme)

http://www.bodhgayaretreats.org (retreats at Bodh Gaya and Sarnath)

Books by Christopher Titmuss

Light on Enlightenment, Rider

An Awakened Life: Uncommon Wisdom from Everyday Experience, Shambhala

Transforming Our Terror: A Spiritual Approach to Making Sense of Senseless Tragedy, Godsfield Press

Tenzin Robert Thurman

Tibet House US

22 West 15th Street

New York NY 10011

USA

Telephone: +1 212-807-0563

Websites: http://www.bobthurman.com and http://www.tibethouse.org

Selected books by Robert Thurman

Infinite Life: Seven Virtues for Living Well, Riverhead Books

Inner Revolution: Life, Liberty, and the Pursuit of Real Happiness, Rider

Anger: The Seven Deadly Sins, Oxford University Press

The Tibetan Book of the Dead, Bantam

The Holy Teaching of Vimalakirti: A Mahayana Scripture, Motilal Banarsidass
The Jewel Tree of Tibet: The Enlightenment Engine of Tibetan Buddhism, Simon & Schuster

Robert Sachs

PO Box 13753

San Luis Obispo CA 93405

USA

Telephone/Fax: +1 805-543-9291

Email: passion8@earthlink.net

Website: http://www.DiamondWayAyurveda.com

Selected works by Robert Sachs

Tibetan Ayurveda: Health Secrets From The Roof of The World, Inner Traditions Bear and Company

The Passionate Buddha: Wisdom on Intimacy and Enduring Love, Inner Traditions Bear and Company

Perfect Endings: A Conscious Approach to Dying and Death, Inner Traditions Bear and Company

Rebirth Into Pure Land: A True Story of Birth, Death, and Transformation, Zivah

The Buddha at War: Peaceful Heart, Courageous Action in Troubled Times, Watkins